CW00741829

TWO MASTERS

The Buddha and Jesus

J. Duncan M. Derrett trained successively in classics and as an historian, an Indologist and a biblical scholar, and has taught in each capacity. He holds doctorates in each Faculty, but is no preacher. He approaches comparative religion in a spirit of enquiry, asking why great teachers were listened to. The culmination of a life's study appeared as *The Sermon on the Mount: A Manual for Living* (Pilkington Press, 1994).

TWO MASTERS

The Buddha and Jesus

J. Duncan M. Derrett

Pilkington Press

By The Same Author

The Hoysalas (Madras: Oxford University Press)

Religion, Law and the State in India (London: Faber & Faber)

Bhāruci's Commentary on the Manu-Smriti (Wiesbaden: Steiner)

Law in the New Testament (London: Darton, Longman & Todd)

Jesus's Audience (London: Darton, Longman & Todd)

Essays in Classical and Modern Hindu Law, 4 vols. (Leiden: Brill)

A Textbook for Novices. Jayarakshita's 'Perspicuous Commentary' (Turin: Indologica Taurinensia, CESMEO)

Studies in the New Testament, 6 vols. (Leiden: Brill)

Recht und Religion im Neuen Testament (bis zum Jahr 135). In: W. Schluchter, ed., *Max Webers Sicht des antiken Christentums* (Frankfurt: Suhrkamp, 1985), 317–62.

The Sermon on the Mount. A Manual for Living (Northampton: Pilkington)

First Published 1995
by Pilkington Press Ltd
Yelvertoft Manor
Northamptonshire NN6 7LF

© J.D.M. Derrett (*1922) 1995

ISBN 1 899044 09 4

Produced, Designed and Typeset by
A.H. Jolly (Editorial) Ltd
Yelvertoft Manor
Northamptonshire NN6 7LF

Printed in Great Britain by Balding + Mansell

CONTENTS

PART ONE
Gotama Buddha

PART TWO
Jesus of Nazareth

PART THREE
Contrasts & Similarities

PART FOUR
Conclusion

LIST OF ILLUSTRATIONS

ABBREVIATIONS

A	Anguttara-nikāya, cited by volume and page of the translation by E.M. Hare and F.L.Woodward, *The Book of the Gradual Sayings*, 5 vols (London: Pali Text Society, 1932–6).
Ac	Acts of the Apostles (in the NT).
BD	Vinaya-pitaka III–IV, cited by volume and page of the translation by I.B. Horner, *The Book of the Discipline*, 3 vols (London: Pali Text Society, 1949–57).
BM	Edward Conze, *Buddhist Meditation* (London: G. Allen & Unwin, 1956/1972).
Cant	Song of Songs (Canticles) (in the OT).
1C, 2C	First, Second Epistle (of Paul) to the Corinthians (in the NT).
Cl	Cullavagga, cited by volume and page of the translation by T.W. Rhys Davids and H. Oldenberg, *Vinaya Texts* II,III in the *Sacred Books of the East* series (Oxford: University Press, 1885). I.B. Horner translated it in *The Book of the Discipline (Cullavagga)*, V (London: Pali Text Society, 1952).
1 Clement	First Epistle of Clement (in the *Apostolic Fathers*)
Co	Epistle (of Paul) to the Colossians (in the NT).
D	Dīghanikāya, cited by volume and page of the translation by T.W. Rhys Davids, *Dialogues of the Buddha*, 3 vols (London: Humphrey Milford, 1899–1921).
Dn	Daniel (in the OT).
Dp	Dhammapada, cited by verse. I have used the bilingual edition by S. Radhakrishnan (Madras: Oxford University Press, 1966/1974).
Dt	Deuteronomy (in the OT).
E	Epistle (of Paul?) to the Ephesians (in the NT).
Ep. Barn.	Epistle of Barnabas (in the *Apostolic Fathers*)
EV	English version
Ex	Exodus (in the OT).
Ez	Ezekiel (in the OT).
G	Epistle (of Paul) to the Galatians (in the NT).
Gn	Genesis (in the OT).
H	Epistle to the Hebrews (in the NT).
Ho	Hosea (in the OT).
Is	Isaiah (in the OT).
J	The Gospel according to St John (in the NT).
1J, 2J, 3J	First, Second, Third Epistle of St John (in the NT).
Jas	Epistle of St James (in the NT).
Jr	Jeremiah (in the OT).
JRAS	*Journal of the Royal Asiatic Society* (Cambridge).
JSJ	*Journal for the Study of Judaism* (Groningen).

L	The Gospel according to St Luke (in the NT).
Lv	Leviticus (in the OT).
M	Majjhima-nikāya, cited by volume and page of the translation by I.B. Horner, *The Collection of the Middle Length Sayings* (London: Pali Text Society, 1954-9/ 1976-7).
Miln	Milindapañha, cited by volume and page of the translation by I.B. Horner, *Milinda's Questions*, 2 vols (London: Luzac, 1969).
Mk	The Gospel according to St Mark (in the NT).
Mkv	*Mahākarmavibhanga*, edited and translated by Sylvain Lévi (Paris: Leroux, 1932).
Mt	The Gospel according to St Matthew (in the NT).
Mv	Mahāvagga, cited by volume and page of the translation by T.W. Rhys Davids and H. Oldenberg, *Vinaya Texts* in the *Sacred Books of the East* series (Oxford: University Press, 1885). I. B. Horner translated it in *The Book of Discipline (Mahāvagga)*, IV (London: Pali Text Society, 1951).
Num	Numbers (in the OT).
NT	New Testament.
NTS	*New Testament Studies* (Cambridge).
OT	Old Testament.
P	Epistle of Paul to the Philippians (in the NT).
1Pe, 2Pe	First, Second Epistle of Peter (in the NT).
Pr	Proverbs (in the OT).
Ps	Psalms (in the OT), cited by Psalm and verse from English versions.
R	Epistle (of Paul) to the Romans (in the NT).
Rv	Revelation (in the NT).
S	Samyutta-nikāya, cited by volume and page of the translation by C.E.F. Rhys Davids and F.L. Woodward, *The Book of the Kindred Sayings*, 5 vols (London: Pali Text Society, 1917-30/1979).
Skt.	Sanskrit
Sn	Sutta-nipāta, cited by verse. I have used the versions in K.R. Norman and others, *The Group of Discourses*, vol. I (London: Pali Text Society, 1984), vol. II (Oxford: Pali Text Society, 1992).
SNT	Derrett, *Studies in the New Testament*, 6 vols (Leiden: Brill, 1977-95).
T	Testament (*in the Testaments of the XII Patriarchs*).
1T, 2T	First, Second Epistle (of Paul) to the Thessalonians (in the NT).
1Ti, 2Ti	First, Second Epistle to Timothy (in the NT).
Tit	Epistle to Titus (in the NT).
Ud	Udāna, text ed. P. Steinthal (London: Froude, OUP, 1885); trans. F L. Woodward, *The Minor Anthologies of the Pali Canon. Part II. Udāna: Verses of Uplift...* (London: Milford, OUP, 1935). I have however used the translation of D.M. Strong, *The Udāna or The Solemn Utterances of the Buddha* (London: Luzac, 1902), cited by page.

Modern individualism, the pretences of democracy, and the current methods of education have combined to produce a deep rooted dislike for mental discipline... In addition to learning the texts by heart, *we* are also expected to accept them literally as they stand. This runs counter to the habit of indefinitely arguing about everything, and to the ideal of 'using one's own judgement'. Finally our contemporary feels quite at home when called upon to 'express his personality'. Here, however, he is asked to train it, to drill, and ultimately suppress it. A friend of mine complained rather drastically that the Buddhists seemed to treat their minds like an assembly of performing fleas. That is, indeed, what they are doing.

    Edward Conze, *Buddhist Meditation*, [1956] (London, 1972), 40.

Be sober, be vigilant; because your adversary the devil as a roaring lion walketh about, seeking whom he may devour: Whom resist, steadfast in the faith, knowing that the same afflictions are accomplished in your brethren that are in the world. But the God of all grace who hath called us unto his eternal glory by Christ Jesus, after that ye have suffered a while, make you perfect, stablish, strengthen, settle you.

    The First Epistle of Peter 5:8–10 (Authorised Version).

The quotation from E. Conze is reproduced with the permission of HarperCollins Publishers Ltd.

PREFACE

PEOPLE will go to any lengths to avoid thinking. Yet in the lives of individuals and groups there come periods during which thinking cannot be postponed. When it comes to morality dilemmas arise constantly. In the discussions that ensue religion is seldom mentioned, for it is out of fashion. It has been associated with much harm; and religious people can turn out to be sanctimonious humbugs. Yet two great teachers, who have become the objects of widespread cults, were in their own days very far from being that. Each started a moral reform movement, no doubt with religious overtones, and has ended up by being a god. Is this not a sad fate for a thinker, which both of them were? To do justice to their discoveries, to explain their original impacts, to give them a chance after all this time, without self-deception, sanctimony, and exploitation of the feelings of others, such is my present and pleasant task. Doing justice to misunderstood people excites me, and as a practising historian since 1945 (I was awarded my PhD degree in [Indian] history in 1949) I have devoted no energy to falsifying the past.

In the year 1945 I was led by a Hindu youth to what he called a Pānduguha, i.e. 'Cave of the Pāndava [brothers]'. When we got there (it was in the vicinity of Nasik in Western India) I was amazed by a gigantic cave, carved out of a mountain at great expense some sixteen centuries before. It was the size, it seemed to me, of an aircraft hangar, but it cannot have been quite as large as that. In the darkness, in an atmosphere created by bats, one could make out a stone representation of an artificial, highly decorated mound (a *stūpa*) fronted by a gigantic figure seated cross-legged, flanked by standing attendants of much the same proportions. My guide told me that these were three of the brothers of the ancient legend, the *Mahābhārata*.

Instantly a heap of rags in a dark corner chirped up in perfect English, 'Sir, the boy is misleading you. The central figure is the Lord Buddha, and the others are Bodhisattvas.' Bodhisattvas are beings, in the Mahāyāna version of the Buddhist faith, who have reached buddhahood (perfect enlightenment) subject to a vow to assist an infinite number of people along the same path. I entered into conversation with those rags, which turned out to be an ascetic, a fakir, a BA of Punjab University who had handed his wife and children over to his elder brother, given away his cycle and his shoes, and set out. I asked him what his object was. 'Sir,' he said, 'I have no object and no motive. I go and visit holy places though I do not know in advance which I shall visit. The villagers are kind. In some villages I receive bread, in some *ghī* [butter] also. I never ask for anything. I simply sit, and they come.' I asked him his age and he seemed much younger. He caused my scalp to shrink, the sensation we call 'the hair standing on end'. I have not forgotten him, a real person (and how many unreal people I have met since!); nor that cave, cut with such effort, and with such decorative elaboration, to house a monastery that had passed away so long ago that even the names of the figures represented had been forgotten in the locality. The Buddha had been reabsorbed into Hinduism; and when my wife was given a beautiful ivory Buddha by a hostess of ours much later the donor believed the figure was that of a Hindu saint.

In the same year 1945 I had stumbled over a passage in St John's Gospel. I was reading it in Hindi to improve my knowledge of that language. I did not know then that St John's, the Fourth Gospel, had percolated through into India itself, possibly not long after it was published. But meanwhile I stumbled over Chapter 14, verse 6 (*J 14:6*), which reads, 'I am the Way, the Truth, and the Life. No one comes to the Father [i.e. God] except through me.' In India Christianity has always been looked upon as a foreign religion, and, located as I was in that region, I could hardly believe that Jesus, a Galilean artisan, could seriously have claimed that he alone was, even at the moment of speaking, the only way to God. In the Fourth Gospel Jesus is well on the way to being deified (see p. 89). That places a very heavy burden on his words as reported, if they were reported responsibly. I was not so disposed then as to believe that people who worshipped him were in possession, entire possession, of what was right. The year 1945 was not a good year to be persuaded of that.

Jesus had been absorbed into Christian religiosity. I already realized that people are not deified for their own advantage. It is to suit priests, architects, sculptors, plasterers, painters, musicians, and, last but not least, accountants. There is a Hindu inscription about 700 years old in which a government minister tells how he set up an idol in his father's name, built a small temple for it, endowed the same with lands, appointed his sister as manager, and his brother-in-law as accountant. Nobody thought it odd, and indeed he understood himself to have acquired merit (hence the inscription). His appointees were given superb salaries charged on that tax-free endowment. If institutional religion is not profitable there is little point in it. Meanwhile, where does moral teaching come in?

Both Jesus and the Buddha are believed to have walked on water. In that case their teachings should have been perfect: they could have had little excuse for mistakes. Even in 1945 I wanted to find out what those Masters were about. When I returned to Oxford I began to question a new friend (Mr M.B. Foster, Student of Christ Church) about passages in St John. No doubt these were naive questions. He showed great impatience with me: I was an 'uninformed' person querying matters on which the learned had reached conclusions long before I was born.[1] When the time came for my lectures on the Wilde foundation in

---

1 I had not then read Thomas Hardy, *Jude the Obscure* (1895), pt.2, ch.6 (Dr Tetuphenay's letter).

Oxford, lectures devoted to religious discipline, I realized that the learned made it a point of honour not to agree with each other, and amongst their colleagues distributed the epithets 'wrong', 'quite wrong', or 'absolutely wrong'. Foster took his own life (not entirely on that account), and I lost an interesting friend. We never pursued a question on which Christianity hangs.

In this present book I attempt to do justice to the Buddha as a teacher in his own time, and to Jesus in his – but with this reservation. Academics will tell us that the actual words of both are irrecoverable, since they have passed through the hands of their followers for so long. The wine savours too much of the wood. Therefore I have adopted an expedient. I have taken Christianity in its late primitive state, about AD 150, when all the biblical sources were in existence, and a vast number of people believed them, for all their discrepancies, to be substantially true. About AD 150, likewise, the Buddha was recognizably developing into a god, his nature having acquired different aspects according to his different functions, as these had been experienced by his followers. The Pāli textual canon, and earlier Sanskrit versions of his life and teaching, had long been circulating and were being chanted as a cult activity, or read out as entertainment. About AD 150 it is possible to compare the Buddha and Jesus called Christ (Messiah), to see what they have in common and how they have both suffered from 'believers'.

To my surprise, having finished *The Sermon on the Mount* (1994), I discovered that when the Christian documents up to 150 were taken together, a more rounded picture emerged of Jesus' relations with Judaism, the culture from which he himself came. The stark realism and challenge of the *Sermon* had been mitigated, while Jewish hostility to the movement had deepened. The pill had had to be sweetened. On the other hand I began to detect the original secret of Jesus' teaching, and its appeal. Nothing proves the appeal which an innovator exerts better than his being both adopted and (simultaneously) adapted. If people hate or fear him he surely has something. Jesus did not flatter his audience, but many odd people took him to their hearts. It is commonly believed they did so because of his miraculous Resurrection from the Dead. That very ambiguous experience[1] could indeed serve them as an excuse; but that makes it all the more remarkable that his followers so soon lost the ability to carry out his precepts.

And this is a result of a comparison between the Buddha and Jesus, that both had found a secret way into the consciousnesses of their hearers, and were successful on that basis. They later (after AD 150) sank into ineffectiveness, being institutionally and culturally *praised*, without a serious attempt being made to do what they said. It is much easier to praise people than to follow them. This discovery is not encouraging. It hardly flatters the 'religious'. But there is an object more valuable than flattery, viz. to explain what the Two Masters were about, what they thought they were doing, what they achieved, and why they have failed.

1 J.D.M. Derrett, *The Anastasis* (Shipston-on-Stour, Warwickshire: P. Drinkwater, 1982).

Teachers of comparative religion in universities are not expected to do more than depict in detail (sometimes tedious detail) the story, the structure, the idiom. In this book I can attempt to divine the discoveries themselves, in their reality, and to sketch out the picture of their fate.

Teachers in England are pestered to teach a modicum of Christianity to multicultural classes, aware that Sikh parents do not want their children indoctrinated in Islam; Muslim children are to be kept from Hindu and Christian mythology; and Christian children are to be protected on the one hand from the blatant certainties of fundamentalism and on the other from a perfect hotch potch of sects, creeds, fantasies, observances, and scepticism. It is tempting to teach them what all the 'great' religions teach, and this boils down to morality: but even there discrepancies abound. The child of the fourth legal (Muslim) wife and the child of a concubine may be such good friends with the legitimate child of a stable monogamous marriage that the last will, understandably, detect that all systems are false, and that the sooner they sink into oblivion the better. A total scepticism of all religions will result and will last a lifetime – for people rely enormously for their thinking (or what passes for it) on infantile impressions. Meanwhile scholarly books on religion – not to speak of reams of exhortation – pour from the presses under increasing pressure.

Here I shall try to show how the Buddha and Jesus were occupied with the same fundamental problem in similar ways, and propounded a solution to the personal dilemmas and perplexities which still obtain. Most unfortunately the solution is such as will suit no institution, no structure, no worldly scheme. My reader must form his or her own conclusions.

Conventions
Here the masculine includes the feminine unless otherwise stated. Here, if anywhere, I am bound, because of my unexpected treatment, to give a reference for every statement. The reader should train his eye to ignore these citations until the moment when he wants to verify them, as I hope he often will. How often I regret the readiness with which I swallowed what confident people told me as a student! For the Old and New Testaments he should use the *Revised Standard Version* of the Holy Bible, which has appeared in a great many editions. For the Buddhist scriptures things are a little more difficult. Since the original Pāli is available in relatively few libraries (in the Pali Text Society's edition or other editions), I have referred to translations, from which the original can be traced by those already equipped to use it. The translations in the *Sacred Books of the East* series are more readily available than the *Sacred Books of the Buddhists* series, which is better.

In the field of religion self-righteousness and know-allishness are endemic. Therefore any statement of mine can be challenged. A grotesquely enormous bibliography would alone satisfy academics, and we have neither the space nor the need for such here. I have chosen a middle path. I have listed specialist books and articles, from which the academics' positions become clear, along with popular books (themselves written mostly by academics and therefore academically structured) which I have distinguished with an asterisk. Many of these are still in print.

Any reference which consists of numbers alone refers to the last-cited source.

In all my work I assume, without argument, that (1) results do not derive from doctrines (though the Buddha and Jesus, like many people still, behave as if they did), but doctrines from results – that is how the mind really works; and (2) conduct alone reveals motivation – what people achieve is a very good clue to what they intend, even if they deny it.[1]

It will occur to many readers that Buddhists must have had some knowledge of Judaism and/or Christianity, and Christians of Buddhism. This highly intriguing question can be left over. It does not affect my argument and is in any case quite inconclusively handled up till now.[2]

In conclusion I thank Mr Brian Pilkington for his encouraging interest in this endeavour, Mr Alec Jolly for his expertise, and posthumously Dr Terumichi Kawai, who died tragically young, but not before he had been godfather to my contributions in the Pilkington series. It is high time I thanked my wife for going through so many scripts of mine and improving them.

J.D.M.D.
Blockley,
Gloucestershire
April 1995

---

1 Schopenhauer put it this way: a man thinks he speaks from insight, but it is his designs that speak; his own testimony on the subject is worthless, but his interests (once we discover them) solve the question. Dr Reinhard May quoted a passage to me from Confucius' *Analects* to the same effect.

2 Derrett, at *Zeits. f. Religions- und Geistesgeschichte* 41/3 (1989), 193–214.

LIFE OF THE BUDDHA. *Burma* (early 19th century)
By permission of The British Library Board

PART I

GOTAMA BUDDHA
(Born between 480 and 430 BC; died between 400 and 350 BC)[1]

---

1   H. Bechert, 'The date of the Buddha', in Bechert, ed., *The Dating of the Historical Buddha* I (Symposien zur Buddhismusforschung IV/1; Göttingen: Vandenhoeck & Ruprecht, 1991), 222–36 at p. 236.

BUDDHA *Gandhara, from Takht-i-Bāhī.* (2nd century AD)
By permission of The British Library Board

I

MYTHOLOGY

BEFORE we can study the Buddha's teaching we must clear the decks, and get rid of mythology. But mythology infects our materials in several ways, which we ought to distinguish. He was an Indian sage and lived at a time when Hindu civilization (free from foreign influence) was forming. Holy scriptures, studied by Brahmins, existed, much of them visible in the Vedas and Vedic ancillary literature which we still have. Numbers of fanciful ideas were cherished, about gods and their 'histories', and were part of the literate culture. The Buddha did not find it convenient to cut totally free from all that: one must talk to people in an idiom they respect, and move from the known to the unknown. So mythology lies in the background of his thought and his teaching; and it is not surprising that it survives in Buddhist scripture and art.

Secondly, his teaching itself utilizes methods of thought (e.g. quasi-encyclopedic categorizing) which derived from the background, and ideas which were conventional but inessential or unproven. There was, for example, a preoccupation with death, which Greek visitors commented upon; and a high valuation given to self-control and emancipation from natural appetites: these too rest on lies which had become 'received', i.e. treated as if they were data. They were, as it were, shadow-verities. The Buddha's teaching could not but use them, and indeed he found the preoccupation with death helpful. We shall not hastily discard his doctrine because it is couched in culture-bound terms. It is the essentials which count, and we can get at them with a little patience.

Thirdly, the astonishment and enthusiasm which he created – his 'package' was more attractive than his rivals' – set off a long tradition of myth-making about himself. His strange birth, his wanderings, his miracles: these make delightful reading, but they withdraw him from real life, and diminish, rather than enhance, the impact of his message. These stories must be ruthlessly stripped away, even if they were in vogue in AD 150. It is argued, on the other hand, that the ethico-philosophical system, otherwise 'theory of existence'[1] invented by Siddhattha Gotama, the sage of the Sakiya clan, called by the Buddhists *Bhagavā* (the 'Blessed One'), can be appreciated without reference to the historical Gotama. So we are cleansing the latter of mythological accretions, and of irrational traditional ideas which were not of the essence of his discovery. I may give a simple example.

1 T. Ling, *The Buddha*, 146–7.

Gotama claimed that he had the special powers of the enlightened ones. These exercised 'telepathy', could pass through the air, walk on water, dive into the soil as if it were water, and so on. I am not concerned how these fantasies arose. Some may have been born in the brains of self-starved ascetics. But we must rigorously refuse to allow our interest in his teaching to be diminished by such ideas, ready as were the Buddha's contemporaries to accept them. We are told that at the age of thirty-five he found the answer, more or less fully fashioned, to all his problems, after six years of endeavour. He, and he alone, was the 'dissolver of darkness' (*Sn 1140, 1142*). Small wonder that he was elated, and his elation was catching. Nevertheless he expected his front-rank believers, his 'monks', to monitor their teachers, and he would have wished the same precautions to be taken with himself (*A 3:96–7; cf. 5:62*), whose eloquence overflowed with an embarrassing variety of expressions. We shall not allow his teaching to be enmeshed in lies, however dramatic. Centuries after his death he was said to have described himself as the First, the Greatest,[1] like Vedic gods, unsurpassable, worthy of homage. So people's indebtedness to him expressed itself. But none of that does anything for his teaching, which must stand up, if it can, without it.

Similarly he was used to talking about heavens and hells (*A 1:33; M 1:376–7*). Neither of these picturesque ideas has ever been proved to relate to anything concrete. He himself insisted that delusion imperils moral development. Obviously it does. We shall strip his message of this whitewash of lies, and it will lose nothing. He himself explained that a *buddha* (a fully enlightened one) must speak in the idiom of the world, without being led astray by it (*D 2:202*). He did not guarantee the truth of some idioms, we can call them Hindu idioms, which he commonly used.

The Idea of Rebirth

A prime illustration of an idiom which must be taken in good part is the assumption by the Buddha that ethics depend on a desire to avoid being born again in this world. He himself could say how a friend of his had been reborn (much as I can say that a recently deceased friend is 'well'). He could tell his own previous births. The widespread superstition of reincarnation offers an 'explanation' for many phenomena, and it also offers hope to the depressed and the oppressed, and a threat to wrongdoers, for they will be reborn in horrible hells, or in horrible forms. But there is no evidence to support it (though 'reincarnated' adolescent girls turn up from time to time), however seriously it may be taken in Buddhist lands. It is an *as-if* idea. Life goes on well if people are encouraged by it in their unhappiness and dissuaded by it from wickedness. The idea of reward after death, or retribution, is deep-rooted,[2] though it has no objective foundation whatsoever.

---

1 Derrett at *Archiv Orientalni* 58 (1990), 310–17 at p.314. Cf. Is 44:6, 48:12.
2 S.G.F. Brandon, *The Judgement of the Dead* (London: Weidenfeld & Nicolson, 1967).

There were a few, of the Buddha's time and later, who denied merit and de-merit, and an after-state. But consciences are formed by association, and by learn-ing from one's company and one's society. One often needs some 'reason' for making a particular choice. This particular superstition served as one. And it is a counterpart to the modern idea of 'self-respect' or 'good conscience' in the case of people not inured to crime, or to practices like head-hunting. A fraud may be financially attractive and one may not fear detection and punishment, yet for an 'unseen' reason one abstains. One invents a reason, and one can communicate it if appropriate. What matters is that there should be restraint, apparently con-ducted by oneself, not by others. One's upbringing and experience combine to produce this result.

The Buddha seems to have founded his system on the general desire to avoid rebirth. One could as well proceed upon a hypothesis that people want to look good in their own eyes, and not least as if they were in command of their lives. When it is all boiled down, as we shall see, the Buddha was not assuming any-thing significantly different. It *sounds* different, but it is not. For the Buddha's teaching was wholly subjective,[1] it aimed at the individual's motivation. The trig-ger for him was the desire not to be reborn: or so it was believed. The trigger for us is 'self-respect', to stand well with ourselves in this our only life. He too knew that one must satisfy oneself (*Dp 166*).

He was insistent that one must attend to the *dhamma*, the name for his system, essential to the good life, the norm of conduct. His *dhamma* was a well-deliber-ated improvement on previous teachers'. In forty-five years of continuous preach-ing he brought it nearly to perfection. People were so impressed that by AD 150 they had expanded him into a cosmic force, or complex of forces. But his actual teaching, along with some of its hiatuses, is accessible to us without our commit-ting ourselves to mythology about him, by him, or lurking in his sentences.

---

1 Tachibana, 108, 270; Saddhatissa, 152.

2

HIS AUDIENCE

OF course, the Buddha knew his audience. They lived in the territories now corresponding to parts of the States of Bihar and Uttar Pradesh, through which the Ganges flows. Races and tribes had left a sediment of populations, an amalgam of cultures. There was no sense of being a nation, and governments varied in style. The Buddha's *dhamma* relates to conditions known in that area, but as they were human beings they had much in common with us. Since Buddhism travelled with speed across Asia once it had reached the north-west of India we can be sure that Indians did not seem so very strange to their racially different neighbours, whose ways of life were very different. Common humanity made the *dhamma* intriguing for them.

The caste system would be strange to non-Indians, but that was exactly what the Buddha discarded for his purposes. Even very lowly people could become saints in his system. Because of caste, however, Indian society had a disagreeable rigidity. Power and competition were consolidated. In a collective society all hopes of reward or promotion are meagre. The rulers and the rich by no means always esteemed Brahmins, but Brahmin arrogance and charlatanry were already notorious. Those specialists in Vedic, i.e. animal, sacrifices naturally did not want their value questioned, and the Buddha questioned it.

The desire to be reborn in a higher caste testifies to people's discontent with prevailing hierarchies. Merchants wielded power; they were money-lenders, and their clients included impoverished agriculturalists, as ever. The economic system must have had its critics, but we hear little of revolts. Rulers required finances for their speculative warfare. Taxes could be anticipated; 'the king and thieves' threatened the cashbox. The legal system (if we can call it such) was haphazard and not comprehensive in scope. One felt at times trapped, existence seemed mechanical and meaningless. The idea of deserting the family, once its continuity has been assured, attracted many. Intellectual and perhaps even working classes pondered on death.[1] To prepare for death was a part of life. Perhaps expectation of life was short. To satisfy longings, to answer such questions, with or without mythology, would be a public service.

There were established prejudices and preferences. People were afraid of old age, sickness and death, even if the family could look after them. They envied

---

1 R.C. Majumdar, *The Classical Accounts of India* (Calcutta: Firma KLM, 1960), 274–5, 437–8, reproduces material from the third and fourth centuries BC.

forest-dwellers, remnants of a food-gathering way of life, voluntary organizations of renunciates. Some of these could leave their wives and children on the other side of 'the river'.[1] Similarly Brahmins left home to retire, as it were, and to die, after a lifetime of observances, ill-rewarded labour, ritual, and devotion to the family and clan. Others too went into the wilderness and lived variously life-denying existences like wilderness-dwellers of northern Kenya today, who have nothing but their independence. 'Fate' was defied, and fear was rooted out. There was a territory, by no means imaginary, where what one faced frankly no longer terrified one. And such people sometimes came into town, to be gawped at by some, and fed by others. They had abandoned the world, and caste with it.

It was commonly believed that doers of good deeds would be reborn in a 'good' rebirth; just as evildoers could expect an evil rebirth. How could the wheel of death and rebirth be broken? For one could not be sure one's good deeds were enough. Some teachers taught that 'knowledge' would save one from that irksome wheel, but knowledge was the monopoly of the Brahmin caste.

Some teachers claimed to have transcended society. Ascetics could set themselves up as such, and had a following. No one seems to have ridiculed this fashion enough to stop it. Hardships did not deter them, and perhaps encouraged them. Some recluses recommended severe self-torture. One could win admiration by it, besides anticipating the pains of any hell to which one might go. The line between psychosis and genius was not as clearly drawn then as it is now.

It is of interest that merit could be accumulated by not injuring other people, or other forms of life.[2] Perhaps the idea was that he who abstained from injuring others would be well treated in an after-life. It is an important superstition for our purposes. One could obtain merit by being liberal, also. One's beneficiaries should, however, be worthy ones (*Sn 463*). They are fields in which whatever is 'sown' produces merit (*Sn 82; 481*), and a status in society (*A 3:31; Mkv 63–9*). If one provided food, however little, for a genuine ascetic, a genuine renouncer of the world and practiser of freedom, one gained merit as one shared his courage and his virtue. It was one form of practising non-injury.

A person who abstained from sex was admired as proving his self-control and independence of psychological support. In a miserable and boring existence sex would play a role: and he had renounced this. He was 'worthy', and one's own status was enhanced by a relationship with his strength of will through food.[3] Admiration of a renunciate's way of life, his autonomy, was so deep rooted that no morality could afford to throw doubt on renunciation as a key to morality – the opposite of our own presupposition, for we are very doubtful of cloistered virtue.

1 See Majumdar, *op. cit.*, under Pseudo-Callisthenes.

2 *Laws of Manu* 6:39.

3 P. Olivelle, 'From feast to fast: food and the Indian ascetic,' in Julia Leslie, ed., *Rules and Remedies in Classical Indian Law* (Panels of the VIIth World Sanskrit Conference, vol. 9; Leiden: Brill, 1991), 17–36.

If anyone taught that rebirth was nonsense, merit unproven, and charity waste-ful, he did not found a school and was forgotten or ridiculed in his turn. People want to be effective, significant, to make some exchange, to mitigate their ano-nymity: and publicly 'making merit' was as good a method as any.

'Merit' is a development of the idea of earning. Were wandering ascetics para-sites? If so, patronizing them was futile. The Buddha explained that he 'ploughed' and 'sowed' in his own way. He and his monks brought intangible benefits to perplexed people, and this was creative work. He himself was secured from ever being reborn. His discovery had seen to that. If he could exchange that idea for a lunch he was not a confidence-trickster, but a benefactor. And tales of his 'con-versions' end with the 'converted' expressing astonishment and delight.

Misers were despised. The rich and rulers who donated parks, causeways, dams, wells, cisterns and shelters were honoured, whatever their motives. The rich were eager to collaborate with an idealistic scheme, though their motives might be obscure. They themselves encountered deprivation and frustrations on a large scale. The rich were acquainted with many torments (*A 1:120*). Their *selves* (they thought) suffered in this life, they would try to do something for them hereafter.

The rich knew how the sense-pleasures, the appetites, tripped one up. Vices born of desire and vices born of anger were to preoccupy teachers of kings. They debated which were worse, for they created loss and all was traced back to *greed*: and vice was worse than death.[1] Tribulation would ensue (*M 1:170*), and this brings us to the subject of *kamma* (Skt. *karma*). *Kamma* means 'deed' *and* its inevitable result in one's after-life.[2] Was escape from retribution possible? Brah-mins and others suggested penance, not excluding commutation of penance for money (an age-old abuse). Gotama denied this. He had a more complicated solu-tion. Inevitable or not, one's *kamma* could still be affected by good deeds, deeds consistent with the Buddha's *dhamma*. This chemistry (*see* Appendix III, p. 130) is not dependent on logic but on wishful thinking, but we shall see it is not with-out a rational basis.

If *kamma* was *kamma* some effect it *must* have. But how could a person amel-iorate his own destiny when the freedom to choose between courses of action itself depended on the *kamma* reaching forward from previous lives or indeed in this very life? True to his reluctance to handle abstruse philosophical questions, the Buddha did not solve this one. But he declared that man *does* have free will, because will amounts to deed (*A 3:294*); and he taught about 'deed', 'doing', and 'will-power' (*A 1:266*). Therefore *kamma* will not prevent a propitious choice sooner or later.

The Buddha's technique was empirical. 'Deeds' arise out of emotions, such as hatred and greed, and also from illusions, and their fruit cannot but mature here-

1 *Laws of Manu* 7:44–53.
2 Derrett, *SNT* 6:60–1.

after (*A 1:117–18*). How they do so is too complicated to predict, but there is a presumption that he/she who is capable of hearing and following the Buddha's teaching can, at some stage, make the resolves and eventually achieve the awareness which enables an end to be put to *kamma* thereafter. For practical purposes *kamma* permits of its being dissolved. The length of time required for such a resolve (a mental condition) to bear fruit in an escape from *kamma* could be as long as seven years of training, or as little as seven days (*D 3:50–1*). There are several Buddhist stories of people obtaining enlightenment (and its effects) almost instantaneously. Meanwhile there could be no other means of dissolving accumulated *kamma,* e.g. by absolution, atonement, or purification by self-torture.

When, therefore, the Buddha gave most of his attention to correcting the visions of his contemporaries, their uncertainty of themselves, and their conception of *kamma*, he was attacking their prejudices whilst exploiting their idioms. This is not unknown amongst innovators in education. The Buddha was neither a prophet, nor a commentator on texts; he was a mystic and a discoverer. The implications of his programme are more interesting than the details, which are secondary. It suffices to be aware that the public's belief in reincarnation and its preconceptions about *kamma* were fundamental to the Buddha's presentation of ethical theory. But we may still grasp the latter without accepting either of them.

3

THE DISCOVERY

T HE Buddha's cogitations must have been complex, but the result was succinct. He used every form of expression to preach it, and this has led to a bulk of sources. But he wanted any person possessing a mind to grasp what he was about, and indeed a child can follow it. 'Mind stands before all activity' (unconscious or negligent activity will not count). His teaching followed a certain design and it has always been found more useful to follow this than to restate his discovery in another idiom.

'Suffering'

Experience is mixed with foreboding. Only nostalgia is free from pain. 'Suffering' includes actual pain, regret, and fear. Even joy implies previous or future deprivations. Health implies sickness, youth old age, life death. The 'dusty' atmosphere (*A 2:221*) of daily life plagues us with frustrations. To acquire something, to retain it, not to be separated from *A*, not to be forced into association with *B*, fear of impositions, all these punctuate most lives. Wrongdoing annoys the doer as well as the victim. It is not *pessimism* but realism to admit to insecurity in this way. Cruelty and deceit may express suffering, and they will cause it. Yet it can be escaped from, subjectively. There is no suffering unless someone suffers. One need not wait for better government of the state to be released from suffering.

Riches often undermine morality. Yasa was a typical spoiled young man (*Mv 1:102–11*).[1] He was converted to the Buddha's *dhamma* because he was tired of luxury. His family was worried about him, not least at his falling into a wandering ascetic's hands. The troubles of the rich include even that. Insecurity and fatalism breed a defeatist attitude to one's chances, and to one's responsibility. Self-determination is rare, and it can be a threat to others. One is free to the extent that the mind can escape. Yasa's father himself became a believer, a 'householder'-supporter. His was a fabulous conversion, a moral for conservative fathers.

Boredom was a form of suffering. The sex-urge was a puzzle and of course plagued the rich most. If it led to life, it led also to death, a form of bondage (*A 4:32–3*). Bags of offal and dung (*S 4:69*), why do we seek orgasms to amuse sycophantic partners? One is a puppet of a natural faculty which ought to be under

---

1 A. Bareau, *Recherches sur la biographie du Buddha…de la quête de l'éveil à la conversion de Sāriputra et de Maudgalyāyana* (Paris: École Française d'Extrême-Orient, 1963), 199–228.

one's own control. Over-indulgence in coitus created problems for rulers and the rich.[1] Women's jealousies were proverbial and even criminal. How could one escape? The cosseted 'lover' asks, 'Why bother?' Harlots ask some 'nuns' at their bathing-place, 'Why not postpone chastity till you are old? Passions exist to be enjoyed' (*Mv 2:222–3*). Too true. And this also is suffering, for the harlots were slaves of their own desires (mostly vanity).

Buddhist texts enjoy relating the barbarities of executioners (*A 2:126*). Must that go on for ever – a useless demonstration of incompetence by government and public alike? But to all this there is, says the Buddha, an answer.

The Truths

All attempts to escape from suffering up to his time were futile, and most of his rivals admitted this. He discovered an escape by way of the following formula (*D 1:255; S 5:361–2;* cf. *D 2:27*). Accept that and one could continue to live happily.

1. Life from birth to death is involved in suffering.
2. Suffering arises from 'thirst', i.e. recurrent craving and desire (*S 5:357*).
3. Everything ceases, therefore suffering must cease (*D 1:135; M 3:280*).
4. To cause suffering to cease one extinguishes 'thirst'; and this is done by treading a certain Path (*see* below, pp. 31–2).

The foundation of this formula is a realistic understanding that desire (to have more, to do better, etc.) does not end suffering; it is likely to increase it. One's complaints lead, if one is not educated, to ever more attempts to overcome the obstacles, and this places one in a circle of suffering. Craving leads to possessiveness, avarice, hoarding, blows, disputes, slander (*A 4:269; Sn 863*). Life without craving *is* possible.

Having accepted the Truths, one adopts *brahmacarya*, literally 'celibacy', but actually a training course like a traditional student of brahminical learning. If a mature member of the general public opting to be a believer, who is conventionally known as a 'householder', embraces *brahmacarya*, he does not have to abstain from sex, except on certain days. His self-discipline is a kind of 'celibacy'. The training has three principal branches: training concerning the impermanence of everything (a statement of fact one is reluctant to accept), training concerning pain (which again one tries to rebut with invincible optimism), and training concerning the fact that there really is no 'self' (a fact, alas, which is the hardest of all to swallow).

If craving is eliminated, one ceases to be attached to people and things. One ceases to discriminate between people (*BM 128–9*). If one has nothing to expect but old age, sickness and death, one can remedy this by self-restraint in body, speech, and thought (*A 1:138–9*). One can at least do this much about it. By

---

1 Gerrit Bos, 'Maimonides on the preservation of health,' *JRAS*, ser. 3, 4/2 (1994), 213–35, at pp. 229–31.

eliminating craving one frees oneself from a set of intoxicating or infectious conditions, listed somewhat awkwardly (*D 1:200–1*): belief in a self; doubts about the *dhamma*; belief in observances (*see* below, p. 45); sensual lust; ill will; craving for existence; conceit; worry; and last but not least, ignorance. It is the last which causes suffering, if we assume pain, naturally, to be subjective. What we should treat with sedatives and 'happy pills' the Buddha treated with a caustic realism.

He had wondered what hampered enlightenment. This was the answer. The mind was bound by five fetters which tied it to the world (*D 1:200–1*), namely the first five in the awkward list above. No individual is permanent. The adolescent is not the same person as he was as a child, nor the adult (cf. *1C 13:11*), nor the aged. The production of hormones controls not only personality but also behaviour, and for its fluctuations no specimen is responsible. The self is illusory. We are not to be hankered after, nor do we hanker after others on a permanent basis. A person is simply 'name and form'. 'I speak' is conventional usage. There is no 'I' and therefore no 'mine' (*Dp 226, 367; Sn 861, 872; S 1:21–2*). Suffering appears to occur in 'me', yet no continuous 'I' suffers (*M 1:176; D 2:64–5*). Disappointments arise because the compound of atoms which make up a person have a continuous personality imputed to them. Change should be taken for granted.

Everything originates from a chain of prior things (*BM 157*). Nothing is 'unconditioned'. One may be indifferent to 'conditioned things' (*167–8*). Pride and ambition are based on illusions. If one wants to be respected, and if one wants to possess something, one is in error (*A 4:29–30*). If the wish is fulfilled both you and the object have changed. The matter called 'I' can be advantaged, yet 'I' has changed before the advantage has accrued. Endurance, however, can be aimed at (*Dp 184, 399; Sn 623*), and will-power can be exercised by him who calls himself 'I'. The conglomerate is continually remembering and learning.

There is no 'I' to receive injuries, or to injure another. *B* cannot forgive *A* for *A's* injuring him. *B's* wisely not resenting it does not amount to a forgiveness (*A 1:89*).[1] Some deeds (like Devadatta's, *see* p. 49) are 'incurable', but most can be cured by revealing them.[2] Since the one who does good deeds is not the same one as did evil (*A 5:175–80;* cf. *Dp 183*), abstaining from sinful acts and practising the reverse, viz. good deeds, one experiences a kind of purification. If the world is enslaved to 'thirst' (*M 1:64, 113*), an individual who injures another has simply postponed his chance of freedom.

The individual who casts off, by his own effort, those fetters (above) can be likened to one who has entered a flowing stream. The stream suggests the unpredictability and menace of life. One wants to reach a further shore where freedom exists and cannot be terminated. To enter that stream with expectation of crossing is to be a real trainee. Stream-entrants have given up the delusion of

1 For the cases of Ajātasattu and Nigrodha *see* below, pp. 127–8.

2 I.B. Horner, *Milinda's Questions*, 275n.

self, doubt, trust in observances, craving; and they are bound for enlightenment, like any *buddha* must once have been, not letting the stream take them where it will. The image is of a man who makes a raft and crosses by exerting his hands and feet.

So the Buddha found in his Truths a formula to put an end, instantly, to suffering on the part of anyone who accepts them. Suffering ended, he is so placed as to strive for enlightenment with confidence.

4

PERFECTION

MORALITY is an essential to perfection. The Buddha had crossed a stream. He wondered whether to help others to cross (*D 3:49–50*). The Vedic god Indra had helped a worshipper over a flood (*Rigveda 1, 61.11*). Normally once one has crossed there need be no looking back, and the 'raft' is left on the bank (*M 1:173*). The seeker for liberation has only himself to rely on, prayers and ceremonies being pointless (*Dp 106–8*). The beginner takes refuge with the Buddha, the *dhamma*, and the company of advanced seekers, the *sangha*. Self-torture is unprofitable (*S 5:357*), for it cannot purify one's intentions. If one strips the bark of a tree but does not clean out its inside one cannot use it as a canoe (*A 2:212*). If one intends to cross one must be particular about the means. Even two monks can be compared: the lonely hermit in the forest may be more admirable than his fellow monk dwelling near the village (*M 1:37–8*); but if he is self-important and jealous he is less likely to be perfect. He must view himself non-competitively (*A 3:255*).

Why had 'refuge' to be taken with the Buddha? Gotama used the Hindu pattern still in vogue amongst Brahmins, whereby renunciates initiated students with a sacred formula, creating new identities for them as neophytes. Homage to the Buddha is consequently the first step.

The trainee adopts a code of behaviour ('grounds of training'), a treasure of virtue (*A 3:445*), the classical five abstentions (*A 3:47;* cf. *Dp 217*):

1. Abstention from destruction of life;
2. ditto from whatever has not been given to one (*Sn 395*);
3. ditto from fornication or irregular sexual behaviour;
4. from speaking falsely; and
5. from liquor that interferes with mental clarity (*A 1:191*).

This is a good way to start, since abstentions and prohibitions are popular (cf. the Ten Commandments of Yahweh), being easily monitored and not open-ended. The five abstentions are held to be more advantageous than any animal sacrifices (*D 1:175–82*), while even connivance at any of the five misdeeds is equivalent to failure. 'Abstention' implies the practice of the reverse, fostering life, protecting property, maintaining fitness. This is generally understood, and one illustration will serve. The shopkeeper who abstains from cheating his customers with false weights (a ubiquitous temptation) practises giving them value for money.

Restraint of speech is typical of such restraints (*S 1:99*). One will not approve of drink or cause others to drink (*Sn 398*), and so one should not speak falsely in public or private affairs or allow others to do so (*Sn 397*). If the liar falls into hell (*Dp 306; Sn 661*), the truth-teller is praised. Lying for whatever reason impedes one's quest (*S 2:164*). One who adheres to this moral fivefold code has crossed the stream, is bound for enlightenment, and for him earthly forms of rebirth are ended (*A 3:155–6*). He will be reborn in a heavenly world (*A 3:24, 150*). So a simple moral code dismisses fears of the hereafter. Incidentally one who practises it helps others to adhere to it.

There are other stages to perfection. During Gotama's own lifetime not less than twenty householders did become *arahans* (*see* below) (*A 3:313–14*). One does not have to be a monk to be perfected, *arahan*, a 'worthy one', possessing morality *and* knowledge (*S 1:75*), fit to receive the best offerings, one who reaches, in this life, *nibbāna* (Skt. *nirvāna*), the 'extinction of craving' (*Dp 285*). *Nibbāna* is the destruction of passion, hatred and confusion (*S 4:177*), the extinction of thirst (*S 3:157*). One realizes it, one goes nowhere from it. If one disdains *nibbāna* as a goal (some did), one confesses one would rather be a slave to craving, an animal-like condition.

The *arahan* cannot progress further. He has crossed over totally (*S 4: 110*). He feels no aggression, no resentment, no arrogance (*Sn 515*). In a celebrated formula he can say, 'Finished is (re)birth, lived is "celibacy", done is what was to be done; there is no more being such or so' (*D 2:65; M 3:291* and elsewhere). One notices the use of the passive: the formula obscures the *arahan's* own achievement. He has realized *nibbāna*, unaffected by *kamma* (*M 3:68–70*), no longer subject to categories.

There are said to be four stages to the desired goal. They can be passed through rapidly, as (we are told: *BD 1:271*) was done by the boy Dabba. After stream-attaining, one may reach the path of once-returning, then the path which leads to no return, born in a pure abode, and finally the path of the *arahan*, emancipated in heart and mind (*D 1:201*). The Buddha did not speculate further about him, which is as well, as the four stages smell of Indian pedantry. The sage, however, is said to have abandoned distinctions between pleasure and non-pleasure, good and evil (*Dp 267, 412*). Life is a void for him, and he delights in it (*Sn 363, 795*). We are not told he should engage in good works.

He has renounced expectations, and cannot be disappointed. The programme calls for energy, but it is the energy of the self-improver. Indolence is the 'way of death' (*Dp 21*). Ignorance (especially about emotions) leads to craving, which must be succeeded by rebirth (*D 2:65, 68*). One can eliminate annoyance by reflecting on the value of overcoming anger, on the wrongdoer's own suffering (*A 3:137*). One reacts voluntarily, not involuntarily in some animal reflex.

It is time to return to the fourth of the Noble Truths, which provide a training manual. All Buddhists, whatever their aspirations, are expected to follow the Noble Eightfold Path (*S 5:356–7*), which is not a set of abstentions, but a set of eight resolves. It is called the Middle Way because it is neither grievously ascetical nor hedonistic. The three branches of training (*see* above, p. 27) are elaborated by it.

1 Right *understanding* ('right' meaning 'proper' as opposed to 'false'), a real-istic grasp of the Four Truths.

2 Right *thought*, eliminating passion, e.g. covetousness, illusion and cruelty.

3 Right *speech*, avoiding untruths, backbiting, chatter and dogmatism.

4 Right *action*, according to the five abstentions, and including abstention from all sexual misconduct, and maintaining the positive counterparts, e.g. family solidarity.

5 Right *livelihood*, avoiding all fraudulent and harmful occupations, e.g. ex-ecutioner, jailer, butcher, slave-dealer, selling poisons (*A 3:153; M 2:8*)[1] – there is such a thing as righteous wealth (*A 1: 112; 3:63–4*) and it is from this that the Buddha's monks will be fed.[2]

6 Right *effort*, e.g. preventing evil states of mind and cultivating good.

7 Right *mindfulness*, objective awareness of the body, feelings and ideas (*A 2:223–4*). And finally

8 Right *concentration*, a deep awareness of the impermanence, substanceless-ness and unstable character of persons and things.

If all this is over-systematic and repetitive it is typically Indian.

If we look at this list in the context, not of the Four Truths, where of course it belongs, but rather of the search for perfection, it strikes us that the Path enables one to destroy lust, hatred and delusion, so that one becomes 'unconditioned' (*S 4:256–7*). It is really sad if a fine person can be described as 'He who resents his mother-in-law's behaviour twenty-five years back.' This supreme purity can in-deed be attained (*A 1:7*), and conduct alone is relevant (*S 1:210*).

One has stepped out of the conventions of normal living; but then all the fea-tures of life of which one has complained, all those which make one wish to escape, features both internal and external to oneself, have been turned inside out, to provide the medicine (like the 'hair of the dog' recipe) to cure them. A sombre description of normal life provides the formula for overcoming it. Those things one hates one does not do, and when done to oneself one does not react to them, as if one were senile. To call this 'negative', or 'pessimistic', is to be de-ceived by the technique with which the whole has been handled.

An illustration was given by the Buddha, and is remembered with glee. Some Brahmin showered abuse on him, and the Buddha replied that as he did not need the abuse, and could not use it, he would not receive it, whereupon it returned, automatically, to the sender (*S 1:202*)!

---

1 Jains (Gotama's rivals) were much more pedantic on this subject: Derrett at *JRAS* 1980/2, 144–67, at pp. 149–56.

2 *Sn introd. to 487* (Norman, II, 1992, 52). Therefore nothing savouring of theft may be possessed (cf. *Laws of Manu* 8:340), since there is (according to the *dhamma*) vicarious demerit as well as vicarious merit (*A 3:33*).

Buddha with his Six Disciples (*Wall painting*) *Miran. 3rd–4th century.*
National Museum of India, New Delhi
Bridgeman Art Library, London

(TOP) *The Buddha enthroned in the gesture of teaching. Nepal. c. 1100–30*
(BOTTOM) *Scenes from the life of the Buddha. Nepal. c. 1150–75*
By permission of the British Library Board

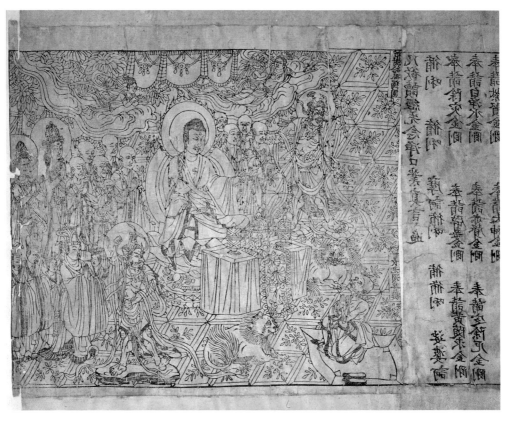

Buddha preaching to his aged disciple, Subhuti, from the Diamond Sutra, Dunhuang, 868 AD.
From a frontispiece to the world's earliest printed book, Tang Dynasty, (618–907)
British Library, London.
Bridgeman Art Library, London

5

MORAL CONSEQUENCES

THE chances of becoming perfect are all very well, but morality is not entirely self-centred, however one looks at it. Man's good may be the measure of all things, but by 'man' we do not mean the individual abstracted from his environment. In what way, we may ask, does this search affect the society to which the individual trainee belongs?

The deliberate actor chooses to be guiltless and to gain merit, if he can, whether or not enjoyment of it is to be postponed (*A 3:294*). He has shed passion, in particular hatred (*M 1:166*). Does this mean that he is indifferent, a social zero? He is not suicidal, at any rate, for suicide implies craving to end something, and he who craves is *ipso facto* bound to be reborn. Rebirth did not take place unless the subject craved for life. It may operate as a punishment, but unless craving were eliminated rebirth could be expected. Furthermore there is no occasion for indifference and neglect of others, since, obstacles having been removed, one's capacity for doing good is increased.

By careful introspection and self-training the sources of bad deeds are ended (*A 4:25–7*). The definition of 'good' and 'bad' is conventional and simply teleological, for the Buddha thought teleologically. Likewise the desire for aggrandizement, exploitation, or revenge is ended, and one's capacity for co-operation is increased. The 'boundless states', sublime states of consciousness which one admires, are really friendliness, compassion, joy (*M 2:304*), with 'forbearance' in its positive form as absence of prejudice (*D 1:318*). These need not be directed towards antipathetical, deceitful, or even sexually-attractive partners – in all of which cases they may be counter-productive. Co-operation is meritorious (*Sn 47*). Free from evil intentions, the trainee puts the reverse into operation. Harmlessness (*D 2:38; Sn 515*) becomes a positive quality. Friendliness (*Sn 507*), sympathy, etc., are regularly meditated upon. They radiate from the person, being realized in caring for all forms of life including the natural environment (*Sn 149–50, 507*). Gotama would never destroy seeds or plants (*D 1:5–7*), which are protected from destruction by monks (*BD 2: 226–9*), and by conscientious householders, not simply as a matter of decorum, or to reassure agriculturalists, but because plants have a sense-faculty (*Sn 394, 629*).

Anger will have been overcome, not by sullen resentment (however natural that might be), but by love (*Dp 4–5, 223*). The word for 'love' (*averam*, 'kindness'; *akkodha*, 'meekness, conciliation') implies counter-benevolence. The primitive

Buddhist lives without hatred amongst people who hate (*Dp 197*). *Hatred* is an emotion that held the Buddha's attention. He felt sympathetically towards the multitude (*Sn 693*): 'Let all beings be happy-minded. Let no one cheat another; let no one disdain another; let no one wish for another's pain...let everyone cultivate a boundless kindly mind towards all sentient beings!' Even kings can practise friendliness and compassion (*A 1:166, 196*); and it seems the emperor Asoka did this at times, as his inscriptions suggest.[1] Whereas one wonders whether he patronized Buddhism exclusively, he actually recommended study of certain texts (not always identifiable from modern editions) and was a patron of the *dhamma*. To descend to humbler folk, a physician may work without fees and have to be protected from his own generosity, as with the physician Jīvaka (*Mv 1:192–3*). Even kindly speech (*D 3:162*) is a virtue (*A 3:30*) which freedom from passion facilitates.

The elimination of those intoxicating conditions (p. 28) is not for the convenience of rivals or nuisances, or even indifferent persons. It sends the trainee himself forward through those four stages. The compassionate opening of the minds of the ignorant to their advantage does not fulfil any intention to benefit specific persons. On the contrary it gives scope for merit, a metaphor for the self-satisfaction of the subject, though the ground for it is 'unseen'. He aims to be liberal, positive, but not towards selected people. Benevolence helps to achieve the deathless state for the benevolent. A selfless person is altruistic for his own sake, not others', for 'good conduct' (*sīla*) is selflessness.

The moral consequences of the *dhamma* boil down to this: intention can lead to death (if carried out into action), to be succeeded by unimaginable rebirths, or it can lead to deathlessness. The consciousness which precedes death is coloured by the intentions which have motivated actions, which will themselves precede post-death experiences (*see* p. 131). If this is *understood,* daily behaviour is modified accordingly. On the one hand the burden of *kamma* is very considerably modified; on the other a motivation is provided for new behaviour-patterns. There is a Jewish saying, 'Repent one day before your death'.[2] The author almost certainly had a similar idea and a similar intention to the Buddha's. Benevolent, non-self-regarding actions achieve that for which every worldly ambition labours in vain.

1 *See* Further Reading, p. 133.
2 Rabbi Eliezer at *Mishnah*, Avot 2:10.

6

THE SCHOOL

THE Buddha's system was one of *training*, not the muttering of formulas. Those that had eyes would see for themselves (*D 3:184*). He never disdained one-to-one argument, yet could teach students in groups. Did he contemplate monasticism from the first? *Nibbāna* and the condition and status of the *arahan* (p. 31) were available even to those who had *not* abandoned the world (ibid.). To attain that stream (p. 28) required comprehension and a continuous output of energy. The 'dust' of the home could form an arena in which such efforts, if successful, would be difficult, though meritorious, especially because one would not enjoy either the company or the monitoring available amongst the like-minded. The supernatural powers (p. 20), even if fairly attained, made no sense in a normal home. When the Buddha decided to teach he was confronted with mixed conditions. Ascetics (professionals) he had known previously were sceptical. He was relatively more successful with those who had not yet decided to make any renunciation, including kings.

Why Teach?
One who has renounced craving could be expected to leave others to human nature. That dusty world – why not let it go on its own way? The Buddha's reasonable doubts were overcome. A seemingly difficult doctrine was to be taught to any honest person (*D 3:50*) who would listen (*M 1:213*), because the teacher felt compassion for the world. The Buddha thought the god Brahmā, impressed by the earth-shaking discovery, incited him. Earlier *buddhas* had taught the truth (it was never without a witness); so he must teach the *dhamma* in its entirety (*D 2:107*). He would help humanity over that stream; the crosser helped others to cross (*Sn 545*), sharing the benefit he had won. Brahmā's intervention does not imply that prophecy played a role in primitive Buddhism. Nor do reason and religion conflict here: for blind faith was not to be distinguished from ignorance (*A 1: 171–2*).

The Buddha awakened the hearer; the latter assented; his training commenced; moral consequences flowed; confidence arose, so that he guarded his senses, and he became self-possessed, contented with little, lived simply, abandoned covetousness, ill-will and sloth, perplexity and worry, and gained joy and peace (*D 1:79*). The Buddha was quintessentially a teacher. One can revere him by living in conformity with his *dhamma* (*D 2:150*). If the hearer's dependants complained, that was their problem. If home life became impossible, the uninhabited periphery awaited the renunciate.

One who has 'taken refuge' with the Buddha is capable of teaching, even to admonish and to forbid what is improper (*Dp 77, 158*). He is not indifferent to others' needs. To his students who became renunciates, bound by his rules, the Buddha said, 'Go now...wander for the gain of the many...out of compassion for the world...for the welfare of gods and men...proclaim a consummation, the perfect and pure life of holiness' (*Mv 1:112–13*). Such teaching is meritorious (*A 1:151–2*).

Philosophical views will make no one pure (*Sn 839*); knowledge about *nibbāna* is not *nibbāna* (*S 2:83*), which is to be 'seen', not 'believed in' (*M 2:361–2*). At the risk of disappointing enquirers, the Buddha rejected metaphysical questions about morality and curiosity about post-death states. A man shot with an arrow does not discuss the provenance of the same before allowing it to be extracted (*M 2:99–100*). Avoiding hair-splitting, the Buddha aimed to destroy those tendencies which were universally deplored. He alone (he claimed) effected this, and had attained the conditions which were universally approved (*D 1:224–6*).

Pupils must rely on themselves (*Dp 160*), take the *dhamma* with them, and so be their own lamp (or island amidst the flood). Grasping the truth, every Buddhist must be his own guide (*D 2:108–9*). Nothing must be accepted out of deference for the Master (*M 1:382*), or by way of inference, on the basis of plausibility, or from tradition. Doubtful views were not to be acquiesced in out of compliance. Confidence arises from personal investigation (*A 1: 173*). In the Buddha's élite association (*sangha*) no one actually 'purifies' another (*Dp 165*). About that *sangha* something should be said at once.

In Thailand it is urged that the *sangha* includes 'lay', that is to say non-renunciate, supporters; elsewhere the word is confined to the monks, called *bhikkhus* (literally mendicants). At any rate the *sangha* could not subsist without the householders' gifts; and it is from the householder body that *bhikkhus* come, and to them again lapsed *bhikkhus* would revert. By accepting gifts the *sangha* gives rise to merit in the donors. The householders' intimate interest in the *bhikkhus* will make them, as it were, honorary members of the *sangha*, but further debate on the definition would be pointless. *Sangha* implies the conjoined monks of Buddhist persuasion. Every member relies upon himself to cross that stream (*Sn 1070*). But each, watching his own safety, automatically secures that of his colleague, like bamboo-acrobats (*S 5:149*).

One must not put obstacles in the way of another (*D 1:293*). Former adherence to another sect does not prevent one's becoming a student of the Buddha (*M 1:59*). On the other hand one could leave the *sangha* under the impression the Buddha had merely invented a dogma (*M 1:92*), or because one found the *dhamma* unsatisfying – that was one's privilege.

Students

It was not practical that many of the Buddha's hearers should follow him into homelessness. As a form of retirement Brahmins and non-Brahmins had for a long time chosen to become *samanas* (renunciates), dying for practical purposes to their families and estates, wandering at will. For them the routines of a household life to which they could contribute little had become cramping; and there was insufficient purity in which to lead a 'higher' life. They accepted alms without being beggars; if householders did not feed them they starved. But these must be a tiny proportion of the population, in spite of the amazing range of ascetic practices they displayed.

Amongst them were teachers of philosophy, founders of sects, to some of whom the Buddha, whilst only a seeker, had resorted. In the solitude of the forest, in debate with their occasional visitors, they might happen upon solutions to the main problems of life. The Buddha's option, once enlightened, to turn from a rootless renunciate to become a teacher was neither anomalous nor incongruous.

What is unusual is that he chose, like his senior as entrepreneur, Vardhamāna, the Jaina ascetic, to propound something like a covenant, whereby the public which supported him, and would support his comrades, became themselves subject to a manageable discipline entirely congruous with his own. They could refuse alms to inadequate, nominal followers of the Buddha, and *bhikkhus* ('monks') could 'overturn the bowl', i.e. refuse alms from householders whose conduct fell below minimum conformity. Believers should maintain all members of the *sangha*, so long as these had not been expelled; but, however curious they might be, it was not within their province to determine who was an *arahan* or not (p. 31). That was an internal question (*A 3:279*).

One could refuse the Buddha's package, and some did (*see* p. 46). One could accept it, commencing the life of a believer. One could apply for admission to the *sangha* as a novice (*sāmanera*). After a suitable delay the novice could apply for admission as a *bhikkhu*. The latter, going into homelessness as a follower of the Buddha, became subject to as many as 227 rules, of varying strictness and urgency. Moreover, he began to see peril in the smallest ethical fault (*A 3:89*).

The believers and their like-minded families are called 'laity' in English, which is misleading. Buddhism has no priests and one can be fully conversant with Buddhism and its practices while in the 'world'. Monks, too, and their female counterparts, 'nuns', are misleadingly so called, for they take no lifelong vows. However, they were not intended to own personal property, save for trifling requisites, or to manage institutions, though this happened in time. Bound by those rules so long as they wore their yellow robes, they could better be called 'regulars'.

The Buddha sent them out, no two together (*Mv 1:112*), to preach. Indirectly he provided them with stable environments, encouraging well-wishers to make them shelters for the rainy season, when alms-gathering and preaching were impracticable. Permanent quarters ('monasteries') developed out of these.

The founder admitted the earliest *bhikkhus* with the formula, 'Come *bhikkhu*, the norm (*dhamma*) has been well explained: lead a life of purity [or "holiness"] in order to attain the end of suffering' (*Mv 1:99*). No other ceremony was required. Sectaries of other schools had, however, to undergo probationary periods before admission to the *sangha*. Caste and class were no bar to admission (*A 4:139*); but experience taught the Buddha to exclude any whose presence would embarrass the *sangha* or bring it into contempt. Slaves, criminals, debtors, military personnel were not admitted, nor youths without their parents' consent, which, in the case of only sons, was by no means easily obtained (*M 2:251–5*).

From the *bhikkhus* the householders heard (and still hear) the five precepts: abstinence from killing living beings, stealing, irregular sexual behaviour, lying and slander, drinking intoxicating liquor (p. 30). These were the *mores* of respectable people everywhere, excluding (say) criminal tribes. Three more precepts were added, but these were to be observed on four days in the lunar month, when they participated in the ethic of the *sangha*: not eating at the wrong time (after midday), not attending spectacles, not using large or high beds (*A 4:171*), precepts which suggest the novice's regimen. Sexual intercourse was forbidden on those days. The eight precepts appear at *Sn 400–1*.

The novice ceases to be a householder. He undertakes to follow the five precepts, the three I have just mentioned, and two more. They include renunciation of dancing, singing, playing music and watching spectacles (which interfere with concentration, distract the mind, and invite lapses). He abstains from wearing ornaments, garlands, and scent; the use of such beds as were affectation of social status; and accepting gold and silver (whether or not in trade). These taboos largely coincided with those binding on the brahminical student of the Vedas. The novice would be recognized as an apprentice of a professional religious body. The taboos will also coincide with the lifestyle of a Hindu widow, a life of penance, as laid down in texts which date back to within a little of our period. After a time as a novice the hardships of the monks' life would not seem arduous. I have explained that the *bhikkhus* were living models for the householder.

The Bhikkhus (*'Monks'*)

The Buddha taught the full members of the *sangha* to avoid doing ill, to accomplish good, to purify the mind, to guard the senses and all mental operations (*M 1:152–6, 227–7*; *BM 78–86*). Not scolding, not injuring, observance of the rules (they were already bound by the ten abstentions assumed by the novice), moderation in food, walking, sleeping and sitting, exertion to concentrate the mind – this sums up all (*Dp 185*; *Sn 68, 78*). To take such a course, to resemble an *arahan*, to lay up treasure which cannot be destroyed, damaged or stolen (*A 4:5*; *S 1:98*): such is the monk's only treasure (*D 1:7*). Seniority amongst them, as with the Therapeutae (*see below*, p. 63 n. 4), was reckoned from 'ordination'.

The monks must not accept uncooked grain, raw meat, female slaves, sheep or goats (they will not be herdsmen or open to suspicion of bestiality), fowls and swine (for rearing), elephants (status symbols), cattle, horses and mares (for breeding); cultivated fields or even waste land (they will not become landowners, live off rents, or attract mortmain laws); and they must not work for a living. They may not dig nor hire others to dig: they will not compete with farmers. They must abstain from bribery and fraud, cheating with weights, measures or coinage, murder, maiming, or any act of violence even at the cost of their lives (*D 1:3–6; A 2:221*). Householders knew what to expect, especially how little would be demanded of them. They would not compete with each other to make merit from patronizing *bhikkhus*. It is meritorious simply to hear the *bhikkhus* (cf. *D 3:183*), and at how small a cost! One must not hire *bhikkhus* to chant verses (*Sn 81*). A monk would not ask for particular food nor comment on what was given him; he would be known not merely by the yellow robes but by his deportment and reputation. He should avoid disputations (*Sp 843*, cf. *800*), and in any debate aim at concord, rejoice in concord (*M 3:86*).

He must not seek self-advancement or admiration; it was an offence to claim magical powers, or the status of an adept. Supernormal displays (*A 1:153*) were forbidden. The Buddha deprecated such powers (*D 1:278*); for the public could be deluded by magic (*S 4:198–9*). To defeat the wiles of the mythical tempter(s) (Māra or even Māras: *S 1:265; Sn 967*) was marvel enough (*A 4:291*). The *bhikkhu's* task, so far as householders were concerned, was to project friendliness, compassion, forbearance.

The *sangha* could discipline a 'monk' for lying, using abusive language, slander, stirring up folk, selfishness, showing disrespect, and threatening, let alone striking, another monk. If such were offences, the ideal image to present to the public is obvious. The householders wanted to be proud of their *sangha* while it was under scrutiny from many quarters.

During our period the idea grew that the *arahan* remained a social being, moving amongst the believers, privileged, almost a law to himself. Some casuistry developed about his behaviour (*Miln 2:84*). He might accumulate a following. Non-*arahan bhikkhus* were eventually demoted in public esteem, and the householder's aspirations were insensibly enlarged. But for the present we must explain the householder's position in primitive Buddhism.

7

THE HOUSEHOLDER

I propose to go into that 'package' in more detail. What was expected of the householder if the *bhikkhus* were to accept his food, his shelter, and the cloth (literally 'rags') he found for them at the end of the rainy season? A mutual watchfulness was in the interest of the householder and monk alike. Criminal monks could not be tried in the king's courts since they were taken to have renounced the world and were outside his jurisdiction so long as primitive Buddhism flourished. The *sangha*, however, was no sanctuary for rogues (*Mv 1:217, 220–1, 225–6*), and a candidate's character would be looked into by the *sangha* itself before admission. The householder feels solidarity with the *sangha*, delights in peace, is loyal to the Buddha, and is free from envy and hypocrisy (*Miln 1:132*).

The householder took monks as examples of how *in this life* (*M 2:169*) emancipation from the round of birth–death–rebirth could be won (*Sn 266–9*). Prestige and worthiness went together. Not the caste Brahmins, nor sacrificial experts, nor reciters of the Vedas were true 'Brahmins' in the Buddha's eyes, only those whose qualifications were perfect (*Sn 620–47*).

> I call him a Brahmin who, without hatred, bears with abuse, beating, and bonds, strong only in forbearance, with that strength as his army [*Dp 399; Sn 623*].

The householder, though he enjoys the sense-pleasures, may cross over doubt, be convinced by the Buddha, and rely only on the *dhamma*. He will not attain realization of *nibbāna* till he has destroyed the fetters which tie him to craving, and therefore to rebirth (*M 2:161, 169*). Those who realize *nibbāna* must have performed thirteen ascetic practices in previous lives (*Miln 2:210*). A rich householder can be advised as to his future state and his needs in this life. The *bhikkhus* show concern for people's good in both worlds, as did the emperor Asoka in his Thirteenth Rock Edict.[1]

Benevolence induces prosperity (*D 2:84*). A benevolent person may act as judge, admonish backsliders, even reprove others, because he alone has the qualification to reprove (*A 5:56–7*). Pride (*Dp 221, 407*), and the desire to subject others to oneself (*Dp 74*), are disqualifications. The 'monk' was not to be servile (*A 3:302*) or sycophantic, though he knows he depends on others, on the householders for his sustenance and on his fellow-monks for moral supervision (*A 5:62*). One who exalts himself is like an outcaste (*Sn 132*). The typical 'monks' will neither

---

1 Mid-third century BC. *See* Further Reading, p. 133.

disparage nor boast of their treatment (*D 3:217*); they are not greedy for sensual pleasures, wandering about mindfully as they do (*Sn 1039*).

'Speak the truth, do not be angry; when you are asked give, if only a little: so the householder may go to the place of the gods' (*Dp 224*). No secular skill will advance anyone in a supersensory direction: ethical progress alone counts. Artists did not often look to monasteries for valuable commissions.

A test of a teacher of ethics is his attitude towards women. Females were then defined in terms of sexual and reproductive prowess. Divorces were commonplace and the categories of women who changed their 'protectors', or rolled from man to man, were known. Classes struggling with poverty practised polygamy to improve their income. The rich were polygamous to display their wealth, while females exhibited jewellery. Concubinage was common in a hirer's market. The Buddha considered whether women should seek admission to the *sangha* and reluctantly agreed. The 'nuns' were to be subject to more rules than the males, and subject always to those males hierarchically. *Bhikkhus* taught *bhikkhunīs*, never the other way about. The Buddha was not optimistic about women's fitness to be judges or administrators (*A 2:93*).

The Buddha's discovery provided ultimate freedom. Sexual activity was suspect because it undermined the judgement. Only a free judgement can activate the Buddha's prescription. Addiction to alcohol and sexual desire are similar. The *bhikkhus* and *bhikkhunīs* must eschew every type of sexual commerce. The householder would abstain on those four days (p. 38), and was taught how to conduct himself regardless of gender.

Which *bhikkhus* were more worthy? It was an interesting question, indicating which subventions provided women donors with the most merit (*Mv 2:223–4*)! Monks were taught: blandishments from women sensitive to monks' potency must be resisted; all hostesses must be respected. Women must be treated as mothers, sisters, daughters, according to age (*S 4:68*). Keeping his distance, the monk advertised Buddhist virtues.

The Buddha did not forbid polygamy or divorce. But no *bhikkhu*, or novice, may act as matchmaker or go-between. The arranged-marriage system was not questioned (*D 3:181*), nor marriages of girls at thirteen. No *bhikkhu* figured at weddings, since lust was not to be encouraged. If the husband and wife observed the five precepts and performed meritorious deeds they were like a god and goddess (*A 2:68, 70*). There is an aroma of conjugal partnership. In Indian fashion the Buddha lists the types of wives. A well-conditioned wife will be reborn in the worlds of gods. Wives can be like executioners(!), thieves, mistresses, mothers, sisters, companions, or slaves. Only the last four types will frequent the heavenly worlds (*A 4:56–8*)! The Buddha approved particularly of the wife who was her husband's friend; her duties are propounded (*A 4:178–80*), not her husband's, except that mutual attention between husband and wife is recommended (*D 3:181–2*). This must be a salutary precept if either will make gifts to acquire merit.

The Buddha did not seek to ameliorate the lot of women in this life, encouraging them rather to work to achieve the world of gods after it. If reborn as *men*, they could opt, thereupon, for *arahan* status.

Why does the Buddha so emphatically require reverence for *parents* (*Sn 98, 404; D 3:180*)? One accepts that he knew at least one parricide king. If one is compassionate, parents will not be neglected, however annoying they may have been. But mere compassion will not serve those to whom one is especially indebted (*A 1:56*). The Buddha was equally interested in the teacher–pupil relationship, proper dealing between friends, the way employers should treat their employees, and vice versa (*D 3:182–3*), and the way kings should abate crime. His words, however, agreeable as they are, do not exceed the limits of mere prudence. 'He who renounces both victory and defeat is happy and peaceful' (*Dp 201*). The object is the correct approach to problems, subjectively.

8

HOW THE MESSAGE WAS RECEIVED

THE householder and his spouse and son(s) might opt to support the *sangha* or eventually to join it, which might be done at the age at which novices were received, thereafter to seek admission as *bhikkhus*. The scheme was intended to be educational, not outdoor relief for no-hopers. An aged novice was regarded sceptically (no doubt with reason). The *dhamma* had to compete with alternatives by no means extinguished by the Buddha's sarcasms. False creeds are not necessarily 'inferior' (*Sn 798*) because they are grandiloquent and theatrical. Nor can they be ignored with safety. But the Buddha's *sangha* spread, not merely through his monks' eloquence, but because it appealed, in due course, to the householders of every part of India, except perhaps the extreme south-west. Pāli sources emphasize the Buddha's personal popularity (*D 3:145 & passim*), but certain places did discourage him and his disciples (*Ud 107–9*, a passage spoiled by a miracle). On the one hand his doctrine expanded to cater for educated tastes, on the other it offered what ordinary people wanted, especially in India and further eastwards. One secret of his success was willingness, which we have noted (*see A 4:187–91*), to couple what we would call secular and spiritual advice together. The common sense of the one enhanced the appeal of the other.

Tolerance and Complacency
Ancient India evidences few examples of religious persecution. Provided the teacher did not defy the state's requirements he could argue with anyone. But did his doctrine challenge commonplace prejudices? People said of the Buddha that he made wives widows, and parents childless, so that clans were in danger of dying out. This exaggeration proved how attractive his package was. Charlatanry was known amongst ascetics, and there were bogus ascetics (*Sn 135; M 3:567*) employed by the state as spies.[1] Buddhist monks were accused of being parasites (*S 1:216–18*). It was meritorious to live on alms (*Mkv 79*), and there are limits to tolerance.

   Pupils of rival teachers brought back from the Buddha news of how their masters' doctrines were disparaged. Individual *arahans* might be caught, tortured and even killed by the state.[2] We must give further thought to that package. It sounds like a sugar-coated pill.

1 Kautilya, *Arthasāstra* I.11, 13–20.
2 Horner, *Early Buddhist Teaching*, 158.

Young men attracted by the Buddha may (with their parents' consent: *Mv 1:210*) follow him into homelessness. Parents and wives might deplore this, but the package was not all loss. The criterion insisted on by the Buddha in any quandary was: will the conduct attract converts, estrange existing converts, or repel those who are not yet converted (*Mv 2:322*)? Many prejudices of all but the lowest classes were reinforced.

The *bhikkhus* preached to believers on the eighth and fifteenth days of each lunar fortnight, at the end of which they recited together their code of conduct, ascertaining that they were pure from all offences listed in it (the remarkable *Pātimokkha* ceremony). The believers kept on the four days the eight precepts (*Sn 400–2*), five of which were binding on them at all times (p. 38 above). The believer is ashamed of sin and has compassion for all creatures and resembles an *arahan* (*A 1:190–2*). Knowledge and meditation bring him near *nibbāna* (*Dp 372*). The *bhikkhu* treats all donors impartially (*M 2:33–5*), lives on a minimum (*D 1:77*), takes only what is given (*D 1:4*), and manifests a model of sensitivity and patience (*A 1:82*). His 'celibacy' is not led in order to deceive people, or to gain prestige or recognition (*A 2:28*). The householder was not threatened by any *bhikkhu*, and no *bhikkhu* hampered his quest.

Meanwhile the *bhikkhus* preached what the public wanted to hear:

1. Status depends on deeds not words (*Dp 51*); prestige does not arise from birth (*Sn 136–42*). Righteous living, like righteous government, *conquers* (*D 3:137*; cf. *S 1:145–6*). There is no conquest like that over one's own weaknesses (*Dp 103*). Even the householder who wears ornaments becomes the *bhikkhus*' equal through tranquillity, chastity and non-violence (*Dp 142*).
2. Being light-fingered (*Sn 395*), sexual licence (*396*), an ungoverned tongue (*657*), and anger were reprehended. Chastity, practised four times a month, represented the path towards *arahanship*, whereas perpetual 'chastity' leads to *nibbāna*, not to the (inferior) world of gods. This is no real discouragement.
3. Commerce and industry are favoured. Truth-telling, generosity, avoiding malicious gossip and anger are virtues tending to prosperity. The Buddha tells every believer that the highest blessing is waiting on mother and father, protecting child and wife, friends, advisers, workers, and ascetics, and being employed in a trouble-free occupation (*Sn 258–63, 404; D 3:165*) such as gives security to dependants. An active man would be glad to hear that.

   The householder must not be negligent (*Dp 21–2*; cf. *S 1:114*). He delights in giving; one may ask a favour of him. He is like a bulwark, like a healthy shower of rain. He is as good at getting as knowing how best to disburse his gains. The Buddha did not hesitate to advise on how to conserve and lay out income in fractions (*D 3:180*).

   The believer is to acquire wealth without violence, make his home comfortable, dividing the surplus, accumulating merit, knowing the dangers of hoarding.

One can be perplexed by wealth and incur censure (*S 4:236–41*). Concerned about repairs and the recovery of what is lost (*A 2:255*),the believer pleases his family, servants and friends, taking precautions against fire, the king, and robbers, and making offerings to gods, ascetics and recluses (*A 3:37–8*). Miserliness is reprehended (*S 1:115–16*). There are four classes: those that think neither of their own good nor others', those who think only of others' good, or only of their own, and similarly those who think of their own *and* others' good – the last makes the best sort of householder (*A 2:105*).[1]

One who already abandons impurities (taking life, taking what is not given, etc.), and rejects the five causes of evil, viz. impulse, partiality, hatred, fear, and delusion, is a disciple of the Buddha (*D 3:174*). The son of a commercial family must conserve the family assets. He must not engage in drinking(!), merrymaking, going to fairs, bad company, idleness, and entertaining enemies posing as friends(!) (*D 3:176–8*). He may opt to seek to be reborn in heaven like the king of gods, Sakka (*S 1:293–4*). 'Bad company' leads one into indolence, which leads to a state of pain (*D 2:91*). Anxious parents would concur. *Disbelief in rituals* is a requirement welcome to those who have no eagerness to pay for any. Householders are praised for having confidence (faith), morality (the five abstentions), modesty, shame, learning, charity (including almsgiving) and knowledge (*A 4:143–5, 190–1*). Morality and wisdom are interdependent (*D 1:27*); so one does not have to leave home, or neglect the counter, to become wise. Nor does one have to waste time getting parts of the Veda by heart.

4. The householder may give alms to 'heretic' ascetics, provided they are virtuous (*A 1:143–4*). A cheerful giver (*D 2:373–4*), benevolent (*D 3:180*), humble, contented and grateful for receiving the doctrine, the householder knows ingratitude to be a vice (*Sn 265; A 1:56*).

5. The Buddha preached abstemiousness, energy, and industry. Absorbed as they were in worldly matters, his audience appreciated metaphors of that kind in relation to other-worldly ambition (*A 4:187–91*). A *tathāgata* ('One who has Arrived at the Truth', as the Buddha described himself) speaks as he sees and knows (*A 2:27*), much as a merchant's word is his bond. Gotama understood the world though he was not subject to it (*ibid.*). Even if the householder did not attain *nibbāna* in this life (which was not ruled out: *M 3: 294*), he could exert himself in the sense of Buddhist striving (cf. *A 4:188*).

6. In spite of their repulsive methods of repression, kings listened to the Buddha's advice. No perfect constitution was conceivable. A king can extinguish robbery by constructive measures (*D 1:175–6*). Republics can run themselves smoothly, taking conservative precautions, not discontinuing religious offerings(!) (*D 2:79–81; A 4:10–12*): a reassuring package.

---

1 Cf. *Mishnah*, Avot 5:10.

On the whole the Buddha's teaching suited a middle-class ethic, and those whom he pleased collaborated enthusiastically.

Warnings of Failure

The legendary life of the Buddha contains many marvels. Ascetics of older traditions refused to be convinced by the Buddha's powers until he flatly denied their own achievement, whereupon they collapsed. But Upaka, the Ajīvaka (*Mv 1:91*), refused to be won over by the Buddha's discovery, and this legend is preserved alongside tales of triumph. The Buddha declared himself a *victor*, but Upaka was not vanquished. What was offered to him *gratis* was too much trouble for him to take up. While Upaka had no posterity, the teacher he was reluctant to take seriously went on to gain leadership of a great slice of humanity. The Buddha meanwhile took no responsibility for his able students' failing to attain *nibbāna* (*M 3:56*), and showed no sign of chagrin when his careful expositions failed to convince numbers of opponents, for example ascetics, who more or less sullenly (e.g. Nigrodha, below p. 128) refused to be impressed.

A *tathāgata*, like a lotus, comes (through the mud) to mature in the world, passes beyond the world, abides unspotted by the world. No preacher of the *dhamma* quarrels with anyone in the world. The Buddha says, 'I quarrel not with the world. It is the world that quarrels with me' (*S 3:117*) – a stance befitting an Omniscient One. But quarrelling there was.

A weakness persisted. Occasionally *bhikkhus* created scandals. On his deathbed the Buddha ordered the boycott of the egotistical Channa. Youths renounced their training and turned to 'low things' (*S 2:147*). Nanda, half-brother of Gotama, had charm and hankered after the world, not excluding the concubine he had left. His colleagues twitted him as a 'mean person' because he adopted the 'religious' life in expectation of enjoying, in his next life, the 500 pink-footed celestial nymphs whom Gotama had humorously promised him. The Buddha reassured them: Nanda was a former clansman, strong, handsome, passionate; but he too had come to the decision, 'There shall not flow in upon me covetousness, discontent, evil or any unrighteous state' (*S 2:191*), and 'he will eat only so much as will sustain his body'. When Nanda (aware of what it had cost him) in due course became an *arahan*, he released the Buddha from the promise of the 500 nymphs.[1]

---

1 *Udāna*, 30–2.

9

THE COST

MIXED motives were not the only obstacle to success. During the forty-five years the Buddha was preaching he never lacked hearers, believers, or (save at the beginning) *bhikkhus*. He never pretended his message was easy to apply, but if the difficulties lay deep they must be exposed with a rigour worthy of his effort. The most formidable obstacle was people's disinclination to believe they had no 'selves'. They did not want to 'be no more' (*M 1:175*). Hinduism taught 'there will be no time when we shall cease to be'.[1]

Vicarious Merit and Corruption
Householders would not have supported 'monks' and novices unless they had believed they shared in the merit of the *sangha*. That merit did not lie, principally, in the monks' renunciation, their consuming little, their reducing the population, and therefore fragmentation of agricultural holdings by inheritance or partition. It lay in their striving thereby for the deathless state whilst communicating to the world the secret of that striving. The possibility of partaking in that merit at second hand (*A 1:151*) is an absolute absurdity, though it guaranteed the householders' respectability. It conforms to an ancient superstition which appears to have a logical basis, since the benefits of a Vedic sacrifice belong to the one who hires the priests.

Those who maintain others can claim they share the merit of the latter's work.[2] An analogous idea is that qualities 'rub off' by association on a person who does not have them; and this goes so far that proximity to the meritorious person or to some thing intimately connected with him/her itself conveys an unseen advantage. So those who sacrificed little (they gave up adultery, theft, lying, etc.) could share in the merit of those who sacrificed much (sex, ambition, prestige, etc.). When *bhikkhus* transferred their merit solemnly to those who maintained them, or indeed others, living and dead, the idea would not have struck the Buddha as absurd. A mother's merit could save her son from hell (*Mkv 32[a]*).

The weakness of 'vicarious merit' lies in the possibility that people with no intention of correcting their lifestyles seek to obtain a share in others' merit in

---

1 *Bhagavadgītā* 2:12.

2 Cf. *Mishnah*, Avot 2:2. Rabbi I. Salanter (1810–83) demurred: one's obedience to God must be personal, and merit is no longer acquired through others. But in Buddhism even he/she who approves of a gift shares in its merit (*Mkv 32[g]*).

exchange for money or the like. Those whom they seek to patronize may 'invert the bowl', or they may not. Buddhist, like Hindu scriptures warn against giving to unworthy recipients; but who is to say who is worthy? The same applies to donors. A complaisant recipient may connive at what is really a corrupt transaction. The corruption lies in unworthy persons' being maintained as if they were worthy, thus conveying a spurious respectability to hypocrites.

As the legend of the Buddha grew a role was found for Māra, the tempter, who sought to prevent, or at least postpone the Buddha's enlightenment. He suggested the Buddha might care to become a (righteous) *king* (*S 1:145–6*). Māra and his deputies were a hazard for *bhikkhus*, who had time, and afforded opportunity, to be tempted. Tachibana observes that Māra was never converted, however many 'heretical' ascetics capitulated to the Buddha's reasoning. One who meditates effectively may, at best, limit the tempter's power over himself. The 'world' remained the world. A *buddha* can move in it unsullied by it. He alone can authentically advise which courses of action avoid despair.

The *bhikkhus'* relations with householders were filled with traps; for association with women obstructs true 'chastity',[1] which is the foundation of the *bhikkhu's* training (*A 5:92*). The enterprise contained an obvious drawback.

The input must not exceed the output if a scheme is not to be bankrupt. As long as ascetics and recluses demand nothing and offer much the output exceeds the input. But *nibbāna* and *arahanship* are like cheques no bank will honour. The *dhamma* must be seen to be profitable, it must not undermine commonly accepted values, it must reinforce common ideals, and, in particular, must not affront the state. The Buddha was vigilant about this last. He would expel a monk for theft, and ordered his *bhikkhus* to obey kings (*Mv 1:301*) and to avoid politics. He did not question the king's decisions (*Ud 23:4*). While defending his *bhikkhus* he offered no proof of their innocence but warned all parties against lies (*Ud 62;* cf. *Dp 306*). The *dhamma* favours rulers, reducing their labour by keeping law and order for them.

But this is not enough. The householder must believe his participation profits himself, or the scheme collapses. Sources of moral corruption (e.g. covetousness) were of interest to believers, and to rulers, though on different grounds. The *sangha's* many immunities were meaningless if *bhikkhus* led irregular lives.

Pride, desire for recognition, hoards of 'necessaries', food, shelter, decent clothing, such pathetic little desires undermined the *sangha*, which could receive and hoard what no *bhikkhu* could individually, since the hoarding of wealth was a root of evil (*D 3:86–7*). Schemes made themselves felt at the expense of the *dhamma* to increase the *bhikkhus'* benefits. Not all of them were in the direction of relaxing asceticism, some (as an advertisement) appeared to increase it. Again, instances of monks attempting to evade their rules and being detected are

---

1 Cf. *Mishnah*, Avot 1:5.

Carved figure of a seated crowned Buddha in royal preaching posture, from Bihar, India
Oriental Museum, Durham University
Bridgeman Art Library, London

Portrait of a Buddhist lay follower, Japan, c. 1700
By permission of The British Library Board

numerous and show great versatility. One could enjoy sex without contact with a female...There is no point in illustrating these unsuccessful attempts to evade the Buddha's vigilance. His casuistry is remarkable and there was obviously a need to preserve a record of it as a model.

During a famine monks of the Vajji territory devised rules conflicting with the Buddha's (about self-advertisement). Their scheme was condemned (*BD 2:208–11*). A group of six *bhikkhus*, the Gang of Six (*Chabaggiya*), not systematic revisionists but artful rogues, came up with a whole row of offences against the *vinaya*, the *sangha's* code of living, and on each occasion their tricks had to be condemned by the Buddha. Undisciplined *bhikkhus* sometimes gathered a faction (*A 1:66; 3:240, 252–3*). One could make those tremendous promises without clearing the mind of cunning. The kitchenless abode of the 'monks' created new problems which the world could have handled easily. As it was, the world watched in amusement. A century after the Buddha's death monks of the Vajji clan attempted to introduce ten new rules of *vinaya* (e.g. that one might drink unfermented palm wine), which were rejected by traditionalist monks and a schism was avoided (*A 4:10*).

Schism

The Buddha was tolerant towards ascetics of other persuasions, though he knew these were ineffectual. He advised the householder Siha to feed Jains, though the latter's practices were extravagant. But tolerance of deviants did not bring him peace. Apostasy even by *arahans* was not unknown (*D 3:15*).

A schism occurred at Kosambi. Believers had problems with monks there. The result was unedifying (*Mv 2:314 ff.*). Even when the Buddha succeeded in restoring order believers responded negatively. A wrongly directed mind is more dangerous than an open enemy (*Dp 42*), and some putative monks must have deserted the *dhamma*.

A *putsch* was engineered by Devadatta, the Buddha's cousin. Two outstanding disciples managed to stave off schism for a while. Devadatta demanded prominence for himself, and defied his cousin. He remains a typical schismatic called 'incurable' (*M 2: 60–1*). At *A 3:112* those who embroil the *sangha* are declared incurable, along with matricides, parricides, slayers of *arahans*, and those that draw blood from a *tathāgata*. Devadatta was predicted to be doomed to a hell for an Age, and fumed at this news. The Milindapañha (1:296) says he was swallowed up by the earth,[1] but his schismatical *sangha* survived for centuries, owing no allegiance to Gotama (which explains the relentless propaganda against him by Theravādins [p. 51]).

Meanwhile Brahmins exclaimed that the Buddha presumed to 'purify' all four

---

1 Cf. Holy Bible, *Num 16:29–31; 26:10*, a startling parallel. A total of five contemporaries of the Buddha 'entered the great earth' for offending against him (*Miln 1:141–2*).

classes of the population; the distinction between 'clean' classes and labourers and scavengers was obliterated. Brahmins, who *believed* without *seeing* (*M 2:360*), urged householders not to give to those who rejected gods (as understood in the ancient religion), sacrifices, an indwelling or overarching Spirit or a soul. The fear of selflessness was ubiquitous. The Buddha owed no respect to anyone, he conciliated none, and the Brahmins' interested scorn bounced off him (*S 1:201–2*). Heretics plotted against him and poached his students as he poached theirs.

Buddhism rejected ceremonies in general, and therefore denied tenets upon which a great part of the income of Benares was based. He was not welcome there, and rulers who believed themselves upheld by theistic doctrines and sacrifices were sceptical of him. What are called deontological ethics appealed to them. They could lay down injunctions for people, and the Buddha had no time for that. His rejection of ritual bathing, so common in India, not only downgraded the River Ganges, but also undermined a basic human desire (App. I below), whereas purification of the heart, and the utter purity of *nibbāna* (*M 1:191*) are invisible. Likewise the Buddha had doubts about the usefulness of fasting (*M 1:107–8*), and other popular observances, established in Brahminism and distinguishing workers (naturally) from non-workers.

Aged eighty, the Buddha was poisoned by Chunda the Smith (*D 2:137–9*) and died at Kusinārā. Women were the first to weep over the body (*Cl 379*). Was the poisoning accidental? The Buddha was insistent that Chunda should feel no remorse (*D 2:147–8*). He was aware of what was happening, the food was (unusually) given to him alone, and we have no means of accounting for the way the (food-) poisoning was arranged. Death saved him from further illness and brought him *parinirvāna* (ultimate bliss) so that the 'alms' given by Chunda was highly meritorious!

The place of the Buddha's cremation became one of the great places of pilgrimage. The squabble over his ashes only proves the power of the belief in merit by propinquity or association. Irrespective of the poisoning, the protagonists of the old religion repudiated any allegation that their paraphernalia were fraudulent and their doctrines self-serving. And the pre-Buddhist superstitious style of monument called *stūpa* was employed to proclaim both the Buddha's fame and his decease, though he had forbidden the honouring of his own remains (*Miln 1:250*).

No doubt the *dhamma* would be the monks' *satthar* (Master) thereafter (*D 2:171*). Subhadda said, 'We are well rid of the Great Samana…Now we can do what we like' (*ibid. 184*). Conformity to the *dhamma* honoured the Buddha, not veneration of his remains, yet Pāli scripture asserts that believers dying on pilgrimage to the holy places of his birth, his enlightenment, his first sermon, and his death, earned a happy rebirth in heaven (*ibid. 154*). Superstition, and self-interest, 'overcame' (to adopt the Buddhist phraseology) even close disciples of the Buddha and his well-wishers. If those he had taught face to face were so unfaithful, what could be expected of others?

10

BUDDHISM

THE world encroached on the Buddha after his death. To grasp the limitations of his teaching we must, in fairness, note what he did not teach, but I postpone that (*see* pp. 52–3, 107). Nor shall I survey the rich world of modern Buddhism, and in particular its relation to political creeds. Gotama, in short, has been found wanting. Outstripping him, the Buddhist world has left him behind.

The most startling development was the conversion of the Buddha from a seeker, a striver, into a god. One could not admit that he had lost interest in the world, or that he had no further revelation to communicate. While multitudes were revering him for the benefits he had conferred, he was magnified into a superhuman being with an omniscience no human would claim. He even existed in various worlds, though he had refused to accept personal homage (*Miln 1:132–3*). Furthermore there arose a distinction between the Theravāda, the School of the Elders, where primitive Buddhism survived, and the Great Vehicle, Mahāyāna. This, beginning apparently in the extreme north-west of the Indian sphere of influence during our period, moved into Central Asia and thence into the Far East, and simultaneously southwards through India. Some householders had tired of the *arahan*, or of the aim described, pejoratively, to be 'a *buddha* for oneself alone'.

Such a believer might well be compassionate like the Buddha, but he was too concerned with his own realization, admired accordingly by the naive. Overall numbers of *arahans* declined (*S 2:151–2*). Monks aiming at *arahanship* conformed to a tedious picture, the monastery by no means shutting out 'grasping attachment'. A householder might prefer to further his own satisfaction, to perceive a Buddha-nature within all sentient beings, not esteeming the achievements of idlers. He began to visualize another type of achiever, from whose (imaginary) example and merits he might already take advantage. He had already worshipped the Buddha in supernatural forms, while the Buddha's 'three bodies' distracted attention from the Master. Now he could study the *bodhisattvas*, beings who started out for full enlightenment intending to help others to do the like, encumbering themselves, as it were, with the slowness of others in a selflessness that reached even to hell-beings, without any engagement with any particular person. Like a *bodhisattva*, the believer could aim to be a *buddha* himself and show compassion to that end. Mahāyāna ethics is altruistic, stressing selfless giving, vicarious atonement and repentance.[1]

1 H. Nakamura, *Indian Buddhism* (1989), 219–20. Below p. 129.

Other developments took place. *Stūpas* (mounds) were erected (*D 2:156*) over relics of the Buddha or Buddhist saints (even sacred texts), and were worshipped like images of the Hindu gods. *Stūpas* and holy places associated with the Buddha's life began to provide merit for those who visited them, and employment for those who served the pilgrims and embellished the shrines. Some monks, subsidized by ever more sceptical householders, began to strengthen their asceticism, ignoring the Buddha's permission to abolish minor precepts (*D 2:171; Cl 377–8*).

Monasteries, becoming corrupt, were reformed by energetic rulers. In India herself further movement towards Hindu beliefs accompanied the triumph of anti-Buddhist movements sponsored by Brahmins, priests and rulers, who resisted the demise of the old gods not to speak of the self. Indian Buddhism was penetrated by Mahāyānist views.

The Mahāyāna taught that *bodhisattvas* had taken vows (cf. *J 6:38–40*) to achieve buddhahood for the benefit of everyone not yet enlightened. Whereas *sīla* (Buddhist conduct) had been a prerequisite of salvation, if one shared the full enlightenment of an imaginary *bodhisattva* one's conduct might be venial. No one need obey the *dhamma*, or be ordained as a *bhikkhu*, though the *vinaya* of the Theravāda survived inside the Mahāyāna. The *bodhi* (wisdom) manifest in *buddhas* and *bodhisattvas* could be acquired by devotees of the latter. The Mahāyāna supplements, but by inference contradicts, the teaching of Gotama; for self-surrender to *bodhisattvas*, e.g. Avalokitesvara, attendant on the *buddha* Amitābha, is an escape from past sins and prevents future sins. The believer, remorseful, confesses all, and begs the *bodhisattva*, in his Pure Land, to save him.[1]

This concentration on the grace of a *bodhisattva* consists with Buddhism's weakness in social and political contexts. For reliance upon grace undermines morality. Buddhism offers to develop consciousness, as an inward poise, and a belief in the virtues, the counterparts of the abstentions. Alas, one can believe, without one's conduct conforming to the belief.

Buddhism does not countenance the enforcing of tenets. There is a relationship between the individual and the *sangha*, or the individual and a *bodhisattva*, a relationship which if it fails, fails. The state may recommend the *dhamma*, or parts of it, e.g. mutual tolerance between sects, and it may reform a lax *sangha*. But it does not enact a Buddhist code, nor does it hesitate to put in place rational programmes at variance with Buddhist ethics. A 'Buddhist' territory may appear to neglect the Buddha's great discovery, even if it passes laws to protect the Buddha image.

Strangers to the Buddhist fold are drawn to the Buddha by respect for his enlightenment, his serenity, his lack of worldly ambition, his devotion to truth. Moreover his teachings appear to offer shelter for self-serving fantasies of their own. Meanwhile traditionally Buddhist lands have no guidance from the Buddha

---

1 Sānti-deva, *Bodhicaryāvatāra* 2.

(still less, if that were possible, from *bodhisattvas!*) on how to run an economy (as opposed to a shop), how to legislate, run an army, fight a civil war, administer laws, regulate (let alone suppress) exploitation of the environment, the sex industry, drug-dealing, and terrorism. Illicit financial gain from positions of power flourishes, and there is no mechanism to reduce it. The Buddha at least protects one from resenting it.

In my view these are not defects in Buddhism. The Buddha never intended to apply pressure to anyone. His discovery's strength lay in its appeal to individuals at a stage when they could use it. Its triumphs have been hidden in the humble, the steadfast, and the quietly submissive under conformism and tyranny.

PART TWO

JESUS OF NAZARETH
(*c.* 4 BC– ? AD 30)

Opposite: PIERO DELLA FRANCESCA *The Baptism of Christ* (*c.* 1445–50)
The National Gallery, London

I I

MYTHOLOGY

I T is said that Jesus of Nazareth proclaimed a form of Judaism, a version of the ancient Jewish religion. Many forms of belief in the Jewish god, Yahweh, existed in his day.[1] They competed for attention within Jewry (which called itself 'Israel'), in confrontation with the 'nations'' idolatry which persisted throughout the Middle East and the Mediterranean area. What the Christians call the Old Testament was a binding authority for Jews, in its original Hebrew or in Aramaic or Greek translations. Teachers of the cluster of religions called 'Christianity' sometimes comment on the fact that Jesus' story and teachings are steeped in Hebraic imagery and mythology. He can be dismissed as a Jewish holy man, like a celebrated rain-maker. As with the Buddha, whose earliest documentation minimizes the miraculous, so in relation to Jesus Paul, the apostle, admits only one miracle, the Resurrection, to influence his presentation of the Master; yet the popular works after him alternate between miracle and teaching, and the whole is redolent of the highly imaginative civilization upon which Jesus attempted to improve.

Metaphors from Jewish literature abound in Jesus' discourse (*Mk 12:1–2* alludes to *Is 5:1*). The evangelist Matthew depicts him as a figure long since promised to the Jews, who were a no less ethnic than religious conglomerate. Luke, a hellenist himself, salts his gospel with motifs from historic Judaism.[2] Praise of Jesus as an emissary from God (*L 1:43, 2:14, 30*) cocoons the abundant teaching, as if the latter were not diminished by the former.

Jesus' 'new covenant' (*2C 3:6*) has been projected as an interpretation of selected Hebrew texts; it necessarily has a theocentric bias. This artistry betrays him. His teaching did not derive from them any more than a submarine derives from a canoe; and the theocentricity, as we shall see, was not total. Worse still, two mythological items, his birth from the Virgin Mary and his Resurrection (after being crucified and buried), have been believed to add cogency to his ethics. This is nonsense, since no miracle, even if incontrovertibly proved, could establish the 'truth' of ethical teaching. Jesus did emphatically commend his own teaching, but not by virtue of miracles. John, author of the Fourth Gospel, suggests that Jesus' *doings*, supported by his Father (God), ought to be believed as a pack-

---

1 Paul R. Trebilco, *Jewish Communities in Asia Minor* (SNTSM 69: Cambridge: University Press, 1991; Gabriele Boccaccini at *Henoch* 15 (1993), 207–33.

2 Derrett at *Filología Neotestamentaria* 6 (Nov. 1993), 207–18.

age (*J 12:37*). The logic of his teaching does not require this, nor was credence given to the argument by witnesses of the events alluded to. John speaks in retrospect, and he will convince those whom he may.

Are there lies in all this – suppression of truth, suggestion of the false? What cannot be literally true is told about Jesus, a respectable entrepreneur in the field of religion; and much is ignored which must have been true. Paul is a lively character, a polemicist who holds our attention. Attempts to make him out to be a miracle-worker (*Ac 20:12*) do him a disservice. His mythology about himself, a man stoned and flogged for preaching 'Christ crucified', is only partly self-advertisement. He suddenly turned from being a persecutor of Christians to become, what was more interesting, agent for Jesus the Messiah, Son of God, promulgator of the faith required by God from all nations (*R 1:1–7*). He, no less than Jesus, thought deontologically, i.e. was concerned with what *ought* to be done (*Mt 19:17d-e; L 2:49; Ac 16:30*).

Jesus' system was eventually called 'the Way' (*Ac 19:9*). How he discovered it is unknown. He certainly studied scripture. Was he a precocious student (*L 2:47*)? Did he have *no* formal education (*J 7:15*)? He never alluded to any teacher of his, and he spoke patronizingly of his former patron, John the Baptist (*Mt 11:11*). There is *no* evidence he travelled to India or communed with those who knew Indian philosophies. A Galilean, he must have known a minimum of Greek thought, since Greek philosophy was studied a few miles away. Ascetic groups existed within the Jewish environment (*see* p. 63), but evidence that he was influenced by them, or contradicted them, is of the thinnest.

He was no longer young when he began to preach (*L 3:23*). Including his time with the Baptist, he may have had fifteen years to incubate his message. His teaching career was short; it is feared it lasted as little as one year, conceivably as long as three years. His reputation developed out of his success as a healer, a success which may well have embarrassed him. His healings were edited to conform to Hebrew biblical expectations, and exaggerated to account for his popularity. But he must have explained his powers to himself, giving his followers an opportunity to magnify themselves. He was said to have been *sent* by God (*J 8:26*): his followers, male and female, have from that time to this sought to enlarge their own importance whilst nominally achieving God's will. In Jewish law an agent may appoint a sub-agent; one ordained in Jesus' name becomes bearer of godlike powers, with sometimes unpropitious subjective effects. For religion has offered, in a great variety of ways, avenues for self-glorification by individuals and groups: a natural talent has been provided with an avenue, matched only by the urge to ridicule attempts at self-glorification by others.

He who does not welcome the gospel and its bearers despises God, while he that welcomes them welcomes God, as it were – a rather naive allegation (*Mt 10:40; L 10:16; J 8:49, 13:20*). God meanwhile intends nothing but good (*Ps 73:1, 85:12, 145:9; Mt 7:9–11*). The Baptist, represented as subordinate to Jesus, announced, as a Jewish prophet (*Mt 3:3; Is 40:3*), the arrival of Yahweh to inspect his creation (?). In preparation for it, it was claimed, John prophesied the coming of a mightier instrument than himself. That the historical Baptist did recognize Jesus as a potential spiritual leader is quite likely.

God was made out to have recognized Jesus as his beloved son (*Mk 9:7*), whom even demons acknowledged (*L 4:41*)! Jesus hesitated to accept a title designed loosely by others; but such fancies would out (*L 19:40*); and whatever the disciples' reflections prompted they must await the Resurrection before proclaiming it (*Mk 9:9*). A Messiah could be seen as a military leader, a possible King (*J 6:15*); yet the good news (whatever it was) must be spread energetically (*L 3:18*). Jesus refused to be trapped inside a definition, such as 'Son of David' (*Mk 12:35–7*), which would limit his authenticity and attract followers of mixed motives (*Mk 10:37, 40*).

His teaching can hardly have depended on such definitions. But without God as his Father, our sources suggest, he could have achieved nothing. His work was God's work (*J 5:17–22*). The illumination he provided through his disciples was divine (*Ps 43:3; Mt 5:14*); his teaching God's teaching (*J 7:16, 8:28*), derived personally from that source (*8:38*). Coy about stating exactly what his source was (*Mk 11:33*), his relation with God was so close that a follower might, without shame (*L 11:5–8*), ask God for anything (*L 11:9–13; J 15:7, 16:24*). Jesus was the world's light (*J 8:12*).

Jesus' connection with Nazareth was thought important: he was the *nezer*, Branch, which figures in Hebrew eschatology (*see Gn 49:10; Is 11:1*). No more significant person for Yahweh's people could possibly arise. He could be the Bridegroom of *Song of Songs* (*Mk 2:19–20; Cant 5:1*). He took others' maladies upon himself (*Mt 8:17; Is 53:4, 11*). Amazement shaded off into worship (*Mk 4:41;* cf. *6:51, 9:9*), the disciples marvelling, not questioning.

Admiration for him grew. His intimate pupils needed an ecstatic vision to reassure them that Jesus *was* the equal of Moses, lawgiver of the Jews, and Elijah, their famous prophet (*Mk 9:4*). Neither Jesus nor Paul after him doubted the status of the Law proclaimed by Moses (*Mt 5:17; R 3:31*). Therefore the need for such reassurance proves the anxiety with which the enterprise was plagued. At least Jesus had the candour to say, we are told, 'Happy is he whom I do not cause to stumble [by my methods]' (*Mt 11:6*).

The message of New Testament texts is jeopardized by Hebrew mythology and Hebraic idiom. Jesus could have been an effective teacher without the allegation (which he never accepted literally) that he was *the* Messiah. His teaching should be judged as a project for the world, not simply as one Jewish phenomenon amongst many. The author of *1Ti 1:4* complains of myths being used to confuse the Christian message; yet earlier Christians had already showed the way; and at *Jude 5–8* mythology is used to threaten schismatics. The message must be viable in the world or it is not viable at all. If it has been rejected over the centuries it is probably not simply because of the mythology, but rather because it has been embarrassing in itself.

How Christians fell away in the first century is not my concern, but if there was a reabsorption into Judaism it will have been facilitated by the new faith's Jewish vehicle, and the consequent ambiguities left by its founder. He did not have a lifetime to hone his teaching. Jesus compared himself to the prophet Jonah and the purveyor of Wisdom, King Solomon (*Mt 12:40–2*); but we are not (in my view) obliged to study either. In spite of *J 1:5* ('the light shines in the darkness, and the darkness has not overcome it'), the world has got the better of the teaching of Jesus, despite the fact that numerous individuals do good deeds qualifying them for the divine promises (*Mt 25:34*), translating mythology into fact.

Jesus' healings, taken very seriously by sceptics, were inspired by his own compassion (*Mt 9:28; Mk 9:22–3*), and activated by his patients' faith (*Mt 9:22*). If the public saw healing and teaching as a continuum (*Mk 1:27*) we may do the same, shaking the latter free from untimely associations.

Heaven and Hell

Jews ardently wished for bliss after death, rejoining the ancestors of the race. Jesus' and his disciples' Father was there (*Mt 6:9*). Jews wished to avoid hell. The earliest Christians used these myths (*L 16:9; Mt 3:12*). They wished to please God and Christ (*2C 5:9*), not men (*G 1:10*); to avoid Wrath (*R 2:5; Co 3:5–6*) and eternal punishment (*2T 1:9–10*); to seek eternal life (*R 2:7, 6:23*); to inherit the Kingdom (of God) (*1C 6:9–10*), and a home in heaven (*2C 5:1*). Some thought souls could inhabit other bodies after death (*L 9:7*); but Jesus saw the righteous as angels *no longer subject to death* (*L 20:36*), and therefore not concerned to reproduce themselves. The evangelist Matthew believed there would be a general resurrection (*Mt 19:28*).

It was thought by Jews that the conquests of their nation by foreigners were due to their own disobedience to Yahweh. For the same cause he could punish them eternally (*Is 66:24; Mt 3:12*). None of this is objectively true, but it influenced an unknown fraction of the population. Another myth was the idea that a Servant of Yahweh, *like a man* (*Dn 7:13–14*), would 'come' and establish obedience to Yahweh in the world as it already obtained in heaven (cf. *Mt 6:10*). Jesus approximated to this myth in adopting the title 'Son of Man' for himself.[1] There is some ambiguity about it (*J 12:34*). He can 'come' like a thief in the night (*Mt 24:42–4*), no reassuring simile; for pseudo-believers would be put to shame (*Mk 8:38*). To avoid these (mythical) penalties one must both agree to obey God, and actually do so (*Mt 21:28–32: R 2:13*).

God's wrath could be remitted; repentance was encouraged (*R 2:4*), and forgiveness would follow, whereupon illnesses might be cured (*Mk 2:10–11; J 5:14*).

---

1 D. Burkett, at *NTS* 40/4 (1994), 504–21; C.F.D. Moule, at *NTS* 41/2 (1995), 277–9.

Followers of Jesus' precepts would qualify for forgiveness (*Mk 11:25;* cf. *Mt 6:14–15*), comporting themselves as debtors to God (*L 7:41, 16:5*), whose creditors they could never be (*L 17:7–10*).

The 'elect' known to scripture (*Is 45:4, 65:9*) reappear not as Jews simply, but as righteous people (*R 8:33*), whom God will avenge (*L 18:6*), another sombre reassurance. They will have confessed to God (*Mt 3:6, 8*), coming to terms with him by repentance, a strategy recommended by the Baptist (*Mt 3:11*), as tradition suggested (*Prayer of Manasses* 7). God (says Jesus) takes the initiative to find sinners (*L 15:4*), and meets them half-way (*11–32*). So he can justly reward people according to their deeds, an Old Testament motif (*Jr 32:19*) alive in our period.[1] Almsgiving could reduce the effect of sins (*Dn 4:27*); but in default a reversal of fates could occur, with the poor uppermost.

That the wicked are punished, and the good rewarded, is wishful thinking. The fantasy is an attempt to explain why 'good' people will choose to do right, against their interests and free from fear of detection.[2] All this requires the concept of soul, of self (*Mk 8:37; Ac 2:31*), the good of which is the measure of ethics. Its existence was not doubted. One's soul's health did not depend on one's relations with others, for one worked to achieve one's own reward. God seemingly could be influenced by repentance. To preserve one's life in this world could be presented as an inferior aim to preservation of the soul for the world to come: this metaphor (*Mt 10:39*) is meaningful only if there is a soul, and its identity is both continuous and valuable. Both assumptions of course deserve to be proved. Romans, indeed, would commit suicide to preserve their honour; fame was a reality for *them* which required no proof. Could there not be an aim higher than 'fame'?

---

1 *R 2:6; Ep. Barn. 4:12; Rv 20:12–13; 1 Clement 13:2.*

2 Josephus, *Ant.* 3.317, boasts that the Jews were proud to obey Moses even in such circumstances.

12

HIS AUDIENCE

JEWS knew the Law was handed down to them from Yahweh by Moses, and that they were the Chosen People. To them Jesus directed his mission (*Mt 10:23*), though pagan petitioners sometimes called upon his powers (*Mt 8:10*). He made circuits through villages (*L 8:1, 9:6*). He was listened to in synagogues; and large audiences were attracted in the open air. Unlike speakers who expounded texts (*Mk 1:22*) he lectured autonomously. He did not send to overseas communities of Jews; whenever he taught in the Temple in Jerusalem (*Mk 12:35*) he could be sure of reaching a cosmopolitan audience. He concentrated, however, on Galilee.

Jews had no established orthodoxy. Stories about angels pleased them.[1] Speakers appreciated nationalistic themes (*Ac 22:21–2*), and the public reacted badly to praise of gentiles (*L 4:25–8*). Synagogue conventions were not a panacea (*Mt 9:18–26*); the Temple as a cult place stifled initiative (*Mt 12:6*). Talk about justice intrigued many for whom the judiciary were a means of oppressing those who had no powerful patrons. Justice was unpredictable (*Mt 5:25; L 18:2*); and public opinion could find a use for a teacher who revived hopes of justice, if only by supernatural means. One who healed inexplicable illnesses might have something to offer on that subject.

One wondered if there was any remedy for oppression (*Ez 18:7*) save revolution. The oppressive effect of Roman rule is doubted nowadays but its impact cannot have been inconsiderable. The poor were exploited, by priests who took tithes[2] and by tax-gatherers (*L 18:13*), who could afford to ignore the contempt shown them by the pious (*Mt 5:46*). The kings behaved as if they were above law, including the Law of Moses. If they patronized the pious they could as easily drop them. Rulers were suspected of being in partnership with thieves (*Is 1:23*), a perennial situation.

Amongst schools of thought the Sadducees, well represented in government, took an unimaginative attitude to the Law; the Pharisees developed sophisticated doctrines of obedience to the Law and custom; and Essenes, with their monastic branch represented by documents found near Qumran, were ultra-pious, distinctly sectarian; whereas, not organized as a sect, the *hasīdīm* ('beloved of God'), if not numerous, practised a form of ultra-piety distinguishing them

---

1 *Mt 13:41, 24:31; J 12:29, 20:12; Ac 7:35, 10:3*; cf. *Co 2:18*.
2 Derrett at *JSJ* 24 (1993), 59–78 (resentment at the priests' rights).

from the population at large.[1] A teacher might opt to follow a stricter school in selected respects.[2] The sanctimony and exclusiveness of Jews in relation to non-Jews (including Samaritans), together with conflicts between schools of scriptural interpretation, provided Jesus with a keen audience, arousing interest beyond Israel (*Mt 4:25*), already renowned for its solidarity. On all sides it was agreed that Jewish ethics were theocentric and deontological – but there was no agreement as to what Yahweh demanded of the Jew.

It was a patriarchal society. The husband could divorce the wife but not vice versa except by special devices; but plurality of wives was rare. Women could conduct business, and childless widows might have economic power. They might be patrons of synagogues and of men renowned for piety and reluctant to work for a living. Religion was continually exposed to the vibrations of family life. The bad taste and lubricity of opulence made civilization nauseous;[3] but prosperity was desired, poverty was without charm, and lavish benefactions celebrated.

Prejudices and Preferences

a. Anyone who defied Moses, and ignored circumcision and the Sabbath rest (and why not more taboos besides?), would be disciplined by the synagogue. Whether actual excommunication (a kind of social death) occurred in Jesus' time is doubtful, but the degree of *orthopraxy* (observant lifestyle) of eccentrics would be inquired into. This collective society accepted that virtue (sc. orthopraxy) affected one's status in this life, one's reputation (*L 2:52*), and one's usefulness.

b. Ascetics were honoured (*Mt 11:8*). Few could obey the Law perfectly in normal life. Ascetic groups, e.g. the well-known Therapeutae,[4] and the sect associated with Qumran, sought to be identified as 'righteous', whereas the conformers with the world were 'sinners' (a black–white dichotomy suited their idiom). The self-styled 'righteous' could save Israel from Yahweh's wrath. The *hasīdīm*, more righteous than the 'righteous' (*Mt 5:20*), were at one end of the balance, as it were, while the 'wicked' sat at the other. The latter were, of course, the 'oppressors' – a traditional biblical image.

Optional acts of 'righteousness', and acts normally compulsory though they were not enforced, adorned those high on the scale of virtue. On special occasions (*L 2:24*), and in order to atone for sins (*Mt 5:23*), offerings were made in the Temple, which received donations even from the poor (*Mk 12:41–4*).

---

1 A. Büchler, *Types of Jewish–Palestinian Piety from 70* BCE *to 70* CE (London, 1922).

2 For example *Mishnah*, Betsa 2:6.

3 Philo, *Contemplative Life*, 48–56.

4 Cosmopolitan coenobitic Jewish ascetics in Egypt (Philo, *Contemplative Life*, Loeb edn., 9, 112–69 [*see* Further Reading, p. 136], citizens of heaven, spiritual athletes, renouncing family, possessions and trade, they obeyed the Law of Moses, but Buddhist influence on their monastic existence has often been suspected. Schürer II, 591 ff.

These observances could all be disparaged as instances of 'works righteousness', but were favoured by the undiscriminating public (*Ac 21:24, 26*).

c. Virtue was considered 'pure' (*Ac 18:6*), the wicked were thought 'defiled'. 'Purity of heart' (*Mt 5:8*) meant honest intentions. 'Contrivances' tended to be evil. One recognized the 'pure' mentally (*1Ti 1:5*) and by a faculty called 'conscience' (*1Ti 3:9; 2Ti 1:3*). Pure people close to God can perform 'signs' (*J 3:2; 1C 1:22*), whereby God intervened in life. Many cultures subscribed to the belief that gods did favours for their worshippers. Physical uncleanness was a model for moral 'impurity'. Even Greeks could call a barbarous people 'filthy', and Pharisees reacted badly to even their clothes being touched by 'unclean' people.[1] Jesus' 'purifying' of grievously unclean people, e.g. lepers, illustrates the attitude of the society and of the gospel (*Mk 1:41*).

d. Everyone wanted merit. It was earned by acts of charity, but Satan was always ready to interfere. This dualistic religion projected upon Satan any unpropitious internal qualms (*Mk 9:42*). One did not earn merit simply by obeying the overarching obligation under the Law relative to brotherly solidarity (e.g. one must not lend at interest). The Law was valid and binding *per se* (*J 10:35; 1C 14:21*); yet it was not sufficient. The Baptist warned against relying merely on God's promises to their ancestor, Abraham, for a 'winnowing' was coming. Tax-gatherers must restore what they have squeezed on their own account; soldiers must live on their allowances; those who have a surplus must share with those who have none: that would be meritorious. *Ecclesiasticus 7:40(36)* warns Jews to avoid sin by remembering their 'latter ends' (cf. *Avot. 3:1*); the Roman Catholic *Catechism* agrees that one must reflect (§§. 233–40) on death, judgement, hell, and heaven.

e. Pharisees invented superfluous customs, e.g. hand-rinsing before eating (*Mk 7:5*), a typical 'human regulation' (*7:3; Is 29:13*). Observances have a fascination (*L 18:12*); but they can have a good *indirect* purpose: e.g. charity, like tithing, 'purifies' food (*L 11:41*).

f. Satan (*see* d, above) had ample scope in public administration, thrones being in his gift (*Mt 4:9; L 4:6*). There were invisible principalities and powers, ruled by Satan's minions, and these could invade people. Thinkers knew[2] that illness was not caused by demons; but Israel marvelled at the symptoms of the 'possessed' and even more at the power of exorcists. Exorcism became a stunt of the early Church.

g. One suffered at the hands of God, or of Satan. The righteous were most likely to suffer (*Ps 22; Pr 1:10–19; Is 53; R 11:3*); and it was believed that their sufferings atoned not only for themselves but also for the wicked (cf. *Mk 13:20; Mt 5:45*).

---

1 *Mishnah*, Hag. 2:7.

2 Plotinus, *Enneads* 2:9, 14.

LEFT: *The Good Shepherd*
Catacombe di Priscilla, Rome
Scala, Firenze

BELOW: *Christ Teaching* (*13th century*)
Victoria and Albert Museum, London
Bridgeman Art Library, London

BEATO ANGELICO (1387–1455) *The Sermon on the Mount*
Museo di S. Marco
Scala, Firenze

13

THE DISCOVERY

No one knows how Jesus' discovery was made. But he used to pray in solitude in a society where privacy was scarce. He communed with God in unfrequented spots (*Mk 1:35; L 5:16, 6:12*), since withdrawal aided recuperation. The discovery may have arisen from observation, no doubt sharpened by study of scripture. The elation arising from a sense of having *found out* had to be handled as a separate problem (cf. *Mt 4:1–11*). Observation has a special value: human experience can be a clue to the ultimate nature of things.

Some existing schools betrayed the public by missing the essentials of the faith (judgement and mercy) for footling observances (*Mt 23:23*). Pharisees, though they may be listened to (*Mt 23:2*), must be outdone in point of 'righteousness' (*Mt 5:20*). Jesus' discovery emerged in dialogue with systematized religiosity. It was not sufficiently widely observed that God, or the gods, easily became instrumental, and almost incidental to the fulfilment of human aims. An 'instrumental' piety is anthropocentric (centred upon people), not theocentric.

Reversal of Fates
The preface to Matthew's and Luke's summaries of Jesus' teaching (*see* next section) points out what everyone loathed, whether the immensely rich or the hopelessly poor. Nothing and no one could be counted upon in this life (*Ps 146:3; Pr 11:28; Jr 17:5; 1Ti 6:17*). If God did not right wrongs in this life he certainly would invert the fates of contestants in the next. The rich here could not count on bliss hereafter. They might do acts of charity, but who knew whether they did enough?

Roles will be reversed hereafter (*Mt 5:3–12; L 6:20–3*): appearances may not be relied upon. The first shall be last (*Mt 19:30*); those who exalt themselves shall be humbled. God will exalt the humble (*Mt 20:14*); for human ideas of merit are unreliable (*Mt 20:14*). A good man's true praise comes not from men but from God (*R 2:29*). Those that actually jeopardize their lives for Jesus and his gospel will surely 'preserve' them for eternity (*Mt 16:25–6; J 12:25*).

The idea is developed by Luke in the parable of The Rich Man and Lazarus (*L 16:19–31*). Lazarus, who died of hunger, will spend eternity in 'Abraham's bosom'. No compassion on Lazarus' part can bridge the gulf between himself and the torments in hell of the Rich Man who never jeopardized himself. This reversal of fates could not even be communicated to the Rich Man's brothers, for Luke despaired of Moses and the Prophets warning the Rich Man and his like in time. Sadly, life's puzzles are not to be solved on worldly principles. The common aims of materialism and opportunism must be stood on their heads, if an ethical formula is to be found.

The Truths

The Beatitudes, with their black humour, lay the foundation of Jesus' ethics. Whom the world pities, God congratulates. The losers will be winners, provided righteousness prevails.

1. Happy are the destitute (*L 6:20*), or those who know they are beggars (*Mt 5:3; Ps 40:18*): the Kingdom of God (and presumably *its* riches) is theirs.
2. Happy are those who mourn (*Mt 5:4*). God will comfort the deprived; the world will not. The mourners are victims, not merely disappointed.
3. Happy are the meek (*Mt 5:5*), who represent the 'humble'. When aggressors have departed, the earth will be theirs.
4. Happy are the hungry (*L 6:21*); God will satisfy them. Matthew (*5:6*) points out that one can be hungry for righteousness (and still be wealthy and a patron of the Church [*Mt 19:23–6*]). Luke says (*6:25*) the roles of those who weep and laugh will one day be reversed. One may compare *T. Judah 25:4*.
5. Happy are the merciful (*Mt 5:7*); God will have mercy on *them*. This is a ground base to the gospel.
6. Happy are the pure in heart (*Mt 5:8*); they shall see God. So *Psalms 17:15*. They are (a) single-minded and (b) free from sin. God will always have time for them.
7. Happy are peacemakers (*Mt 5:9*), sons of God, his agents, for he is God of peace (*R 16:20*). 'Peacemaking' is a contagious friendliness.
8. Happy are those who are persecuted for righteousness' sake (*Mt 5:10*), for theirs is the Kingdom of heaven. They are happy when people *slander* them (*L 6:22*), let alone when the world crucifies them (*Mt 16:24*). Such is the tone of early Church life, for
9. Happy are you when 'they blame you and persecute you and say every bad thing about you falsely for my sake. Rejoice and be overjoyed for (a) your reward (merit) is great in heaven, and (b) that was the way they [*L 6:23* says 'their fathers'] persecuted the prophets that preceded you.'

Although the world will abuse you, you are entitled to pursue a policy devoid of aggression, ambition, exigence. If you believe God can achieve his will your rewards are tremendous. God does not bother to reward those that reward themselves. Belief in God recommends a definite strategy, which does not coincide with the world's. Scribes concentrated on scripture; Pharisees concentrated on observances; and Sadducees had difficulty in taking another world or a spiritual life seriously: it is understandable Jesus was at odds with all of them. To check his orthopraxy they could be unpleasantly inquisitive (*Mk 2:24, 3:22, 7:1*). He never admitted he defied the Law and the Prophets (*Mt 5:17*); he simply found fault with their exponents.

What was required was faithfulness with and towards God's kingdom (*L 16:10–12*). Jesus could require a patient to obey the Law of Moses, thereby placating priestly hostility to himself (*Mk 1:40–5*). If the Fourth Gospel sees Jesus above the Law (*J 8:17*), his precepts must be understood *and* done (*J 13:17*). In contrast to Scribes and Pharisees, Jesus' own precepts were light (cf. *Is 10:27*), for he demanded in sum less than his opponents from the public. But if he attacked some of his rivals for ignoring covetousness, immoderate consumption, etc. – for God is concerned with both the inside and the outside of any 'vessel' (*Mt 23:25–6; L 11:39–41*) – his simple precepts demanded a searching conscience, which could be heavier than observances.

The Kingdom is already present (*Co 1:13–14*), like ferment in dough (*1C 5:6*), in the midst of the disciples (*L 17:20–1*), a subjective condition (*Mk 11:24*). There a faith exists strong enough to move mountains[1] and to realize every just wish (*L 11:9–13; J 14:13–4*). God will refuse nothing to disciples who remain faithful to Jesus' teaching (*J 15:7, 16:23*).

Jesus reprehends observances, instancing repetitive (or babbling) prayer (*Mt 6:7, 31–2*), the wearing of highly visible amulets (*Mt 23:5*), or garments advertising rank (*Mk 12:38*). Paul wages war on those who preach observances instead of the faith which has unlimited requirements (*R 9:32; Co 2:16, 21–3*) though he was patient enough with those who were addicted to particular observances (*R 14:2–7*). No one says, 'Happy are they who perform many observances!' By AD 150 the Christ of the gnostics rejects fasting, prayer and alms-giving out of hand, as as useless as the Jews' dietary laws.[2]

---

1 Derrett at *Bibbia e Oriente* 30 (1988), 231–44 (on *Mk 11:22*) = *SNT* 6:28–41. Signs of the End Time (*see Ps 114*).

2 *Gospel of Thomas* (from the Nag Hammadi library), *logion* 14.

14

PERFECTION

IN tune with the Beatitudes the disciple manifests spiritual achievement. Philo, the Jewish philosopher, was aware of the rational degrees of success in a serious training-course, but he thought more systematically than our Christian sources.[1] *Can* one become perfect (*P 3:14–15*)? Paul wanted to present every convert to Christ as 'perfect' (*Co 1:28*). To become perfect (*Mt 5:48*) one must imitate God (*E 5:1*). The Old Testament required Israel to be 'holy' as God is holy (*Lv 11:44, 20:26*). Some people are already *near* the Kingdom (*Mk 12:34*); others will be far from it till they 'repent'. Those who master and embody Jesus' teaching are both 'salt' and 'light' for the world (*Mt 5:13–14*). Perfection is catching.

Following Jesus is a full-time task (*Mt 8:21*). If his words were a key to eternal life (*J 6:68*) that was reasonable but rival teachers would be jealous. 'What shall we do to be saved [from the Wrath]?' (*Ac 4:12, 16:30*). The answer is detailed:

1. The Law forbids killing; Jesus forbids anger and verbal abuse (*Mt 5:21–2*). Others' resentment must be appeased before one approaches God (*Mt 5:23–4*). God is an adversary who can extract every cent (*5:25–6*). Debt is the standing metonym for sin.[2] One should be ready to relieve others from such burdens (*Mk 11:25; Mt 6:14–15*).
2. The Law forbids adultery. One must avoid facilitating irregular sexual acts (*Mt 5:27–30*). What is deplored is the sinfulness of one who connives at sexual irregularity on his own part *and* others'.
3. The Law restricts retaliation. Jesus claims one should not resist a wicked person (*5:38*), but suffer brutal insults meekly. One should concede lawsuits. Under impressment one should co-operate. Those who beg for loans should be entertained (*5:42*). One's security comes second to one's righteousness.
4. The Law requires us to love our neighbours. What of enemies (*5:43*)? One should love and benefit them, and even bless those who curse one (*L 6:28*). One prays for those that persecute one. God usually treats people equally (*L 6:35*). The wicked discriminate in favour of their 'brothers': one can do better than that, since there is no limit to true brotherhood.

It is a programme requiring insight (*1Pe 4:1*) and forbearance.

---

1 Beginners, improvers, perfect: Philo, *On Agriculture* 159, 165 (Loeb edn., III 191, 195). Even the perfect need practice in meeting challenges.

2 Derrett at *Downside Review* 109 (1991), 173–82.

15

MORAL CONSEQUENCES

THE world's standards (*Co 2:8*) are no authority (*R 12:2*); the 'flesh' is a false guide (*R 8:4–5, 13:14*); those who are 'in the flesh' are bound for death (*R 8:6; 1C 3:3*). To do the Father's will is to live for ever, while the world and its attractions perish (*1J 2: 15–17*). The Father is not concerned to advantage the 'flesh'.

Violence is reprehended at *Mt 26:52*; but the difficult passage where Jesus commends the acquisition of a sword (*L 22:36*), a passage alluding to Old Testament prophecies, suggests that self-defence is allowable. Both the Essenes and the Therapeutae approved of self-defence. The meek are unlikely to instigate violence. Heroes can enter life by a narrow gate (*L 13:23–4*); one is invited inside, not shut out (*L 13:25–7*). At the last, the ancestors are joined (*L 13:28*).

1. Generosity is commended: one should aim to be rich in good deeds (*1Ti 6:18*). Hoarding is objected to (*L 12:16–21*). Generosity advantages the giver (*Mt 6:22–3*), who obtains merit by giving to those who cannot reciprocate (*L 14:12*, cf. *6:33*).
   Whilst giving alms or praying one should keep one's act quite private. If one acts to gain neighbours' approval the merit is forfeited (*Mt 6:1–6*). Man's good, not even God's will, decides here; God approves of that which experience shows to be meritorious. Fasting should be conducted secretly (*6:16–18*).

2. A form of common prayer is taught (*Mt 6:9–13*). One submits to the divine will, denying a personal agenda, asking for no more than bread for the current day.

3. One will not aim to accumulate treasure. One may hope for it in heaven (i.e. merit), where no one can steal it (*Mt 6:19–21*).

4. One cannot serve two masters (excepting the rare case where they are of one mind); one of them will lose. 'One cannot serve both God and *mammon* [money]' (*Mt 6:24*). So a world-ruler must be obeyed so far as is consistent with God's will (*Mk 12:17; R 13:1*). One prays for one's rulers (*1Ti 2:2*).

5. Put food and clothing low in priority. God has provided means for you as for the rest of creation. Concern for food and clothing is a *distraction* (*Mt 6:25–34*); since one's needs will be a by-product of a series of right decisions.

6. Only those free from disqualifications may judge others (*Mt 7:1–5*). The treasures of knowledge are not to be squandered on the hopeless (*7:6*).

7. Reliance on God is justified. He will supply what we need.

8. Consequently we must do for others what we should wish them to do for us, if the roles were reversed (*Mt 7:12*). If, as Jesus says, the Law and the Prophets amount to this, the idea is the foundation of his system.[1] It is important to notice that the idea is not theocentric, and is teleological – results alone will establish the prudence of the precept.

9. Formulas for living must be tested by their fruits. Do they accomplish what is required? Pestered by Christians claiming to have visions (*Co 2:18*), the Church learnt to test all 'spirits', not by reason but by conformity with the Word (*1J 4:4*). Results *are* a clue to intentions.

10. Lip service to this programme will achieve nothing. Successful disciples may in fact not enter the Kingdom, though folk of previously evil life may do so (*Mt 21:31*) (cf. p. 82 below). Success is measured by doing God's will, not by using one's gifts. On the Last Day Jesus will send forward into the Kingdom only those who have succoured the poor, sick and helpless (*Mt 25:34*), thereby personally (*Mt 25:12*) acting as God's functionaries (*T. Jos. 1:5–6*).

11. Disciples who hear this teaching and carry it out are like those who build on rock; those that *hear* and do not *do* are building on sand (*Mt 7:24–7*). Jesus has total confidence in his discovery, which is not theoretical.

I have not exaggerated the defensive air of the Sermon on the Mount. The gospel as a whole has this air; Jesus must have foreseen persecution. The warnings against enemies, rivals, and false prophets, and against not carrying his teaching out completely, show how anxious he was lest the world would overcome him. His sacrifice (below p. 86) enabled him to claim he had overcome the world (*J 16:33*), but without it would he have done so? No rational defence of his Way has yet been offered. Up till AD 150 no one has asked the hearer to listen and judge for himself. Paul says, 'Test everything; retain what is good' (*1T 5:21*); but he means one should test others' formulas against the Word. At *Mt 17:25* and *L 7:42* we see persuasion employed, but that is quite exceptional.

The Sermon on the Mount does not list virtues, but *faith* is very prominent in all New Testament works. Unless one has absolute faith one will not accept Jesus' package. Lists of virtues which this decision can engender or develop figure in Paul's work (*Co 3:12–14*), but more richly in later Christian texts, obviously filling a gap. The need for truth-telling (as opposed to keeping one's oath) seems to have arisen somewhat late (*Co 3:9* is a lonely early example).

One aspect is worked out in detail: love of God (*Mk 12:30*); of the neighbour (*12:31*); and of enemies (*Mt 5:44*). Love figures in servants' attitude to their masters (*Mt 6:24*), and between a pagan and Jews (*L 7:5*). One loves one who forgives

---

1 If one consistently does to others what one would wish them to do to oneself (including the negative form, 'does not do to others…') one abandons the aggressive and acquisitive habits which one deplores in others and is released from sin. One becomes a good servant of God, if such a God there be. *See* below, p. 130.

one's debt (*L 7:42*), love being an aspect of gratitude (*ibid.* 47). The Fourth Gospel uses the word of God's attitude, of Jesus' attitude, and of his disciples' attitude towards one another (*J 13:34; 1J 4:7*). But how can love be *ordered*? In a collective society emotions are stereotyped, like roles. Endless forgiveness suggests love (*Mt 18:22*), and this fits.

Compassion towards complete strangers can be an expensive sort of love. The behaviour of the Good Samaritan in the famous parable is that which Jesus prescribed (*L 10:37*). Paul advises, 'do good to all men, especially fellow Christians' (*G 6:10*), which is by no means the same thing. The prophet Isaiah had long since promised (*58:7–8*) every aspect of merit to those who helped the destitute.

With love comes humility (*L 14:7–11*). Jesus emphasized his humble position as a kind of servant, and (it seems) he even washed his pupils' feet to dramatize this (*J 13:1–15*). The world seeks to be great, but the disciples must serve each other; the would-be greatest must serve all of them (*Mk 9:35, 10:43–4;* cf. *L 22:26*). God himself will take pains to serve his faithful servants (*L 12:37*). But there is no humility like a sincere plea for God's mercy (*L 18:13*), a plea for which God is prepared to wait (*L 13:1–9*).

Humility is all very well, but one must discriminate when heterodox teachers claim attention and obedience: the disciples are mutually brothers, and, while no one disciple is entitled to lord it over the remainder, none of them ought to call any man 'Father' on earth, however charismatic (*Mt 23:8–9*).[1]

---

1 Derrett, *SNT* 3:215–29.

16

THE SCHOOL

BROADLY speaking, the scheme was ascetical. Normal instincts were challenged, and the result must be hostility from the Palestinian public. 'Love of enemies' must imperil national defence, to say the least. And a consumer society is undermined by 'Be content with little' (*1 Ti 6:8*), as the apostles evidently were.

The famous healer and prophet attracted numbers, whose importunity could overwhelm him (*Mk 6:31*). Did any of them subscribe to his ethical system? His recruiting technique was quaint, impulsive. Some were recruited through previous recruits (*J 1:41, 45*), but how often this happened we do not know.

His description of his public teaching was certainly quaint: the Word is sown broadcast, and will germinate according to soil and weather. Only 25 per cent of the seed will crop (*Mk 4:20*). This pessimism fits the unflattering nature of the message: nothing could be more passive than soil. Furthermore, weeds grow amongst the grain, the work of an enemy (Satan?); and they have to be endured till the harvest, when they are to be burnt (*Mt 13:24–30*). But a harvest there will be, it seems. All this is somewhat menacing.

At least Jesus did not set up a counter-culture in the desert (cf. *Ac 21:38*). He did not disparage home life, as the 'Qumran' folk did. It was there, after all, his recruits would win spurs. Was it possible that a confirmed sinner might listen to the preacher, restore ill-gotten gain, make gifts to the poor, and seek social reinstatement? Luke says it happened (*L 19:5–10*).

Those that welcome reformed sinners love their enemies (cf. *Ac 9:13–19*) and become 'sons of your Father in heaven' (*Mt 5:45*). A reformed life is more persuasive than any amount of preaching.[1] And Jesus seldom[2] shunned publicity. Preaching in and out of season came to be recommended (*2 Ti 4:2*).

Why Teach?
After his association with the Baptist, about which we know little, he attracts the titles 'Rabbi' and 'Teacher' (*L 5:5*). He discusses his title, Master, with his disciples (*J 13:13*): he is really their servant. But none of them can rival him. He had been tempted to take to remunerative walks of life, including displays of magical powers – a masterpiece of irony. All that Satan could offer him, even as a 'ruler', he later attained, in a spiritual sense, as a recognized 'Son of God' (*Mt 4:3–11*).

1 Plutarch, *Moralia* 41B, 233B, 801B.
2 *Mt 8:4(?), 16:20, 17:9*. Jesus attempts to avoid unhelpful excitement.

He resisted that worldly 'temptation'.

What were the grievances, the abuses that required to be remedied? The Old Testament is eloquent: theft, murder, adultery, false swearing, all kinds of idolatry, along with sanctimony. The world had not changed since *Jr 7:9–10*, which tells this tale. The Romans' rule in itself proved God's anger. Israel was faithless, and even the best were feeble (*Mt 17:17*). Jesus saw himself as charged with God's message, in the face of Satan's wiles and the uselessness of professional teachers. These would not help a benighted public, which suffered their pedantries (*Mt 23:4*). There was a saying, 'If you will not help me lift this I shall not bother!'[1] In view of professionals' incompetence Jesus ridiculed their prestige and arrogance (*Mk 13:38–40*), seeing himself as a physician attending the (spiritually) sick (*Mk 2:17*), who were the better qualified to benefit from him the less educated they were (*Mk 10:15; Mt 11:25–7*).

He realized that he and his collaborators would be in danger (*see* p. 85). His motivation is stated to be compassion,[2] a sentiment projected upon God as his principal (*Mk 5:19; L 7:16*). Granted that an autodidact's teaching argues a hope to glorify himself (*J 7:18, 8:13–15*), his audience should consider Jesus no mere lad from Nazareth (*Mk 6:3*), but a messenger from heaven to worldly people (*J 8:23*). His status is stated baldly at *L 10:22*: 'Everything has been conveyed to me by my Father, and none knows who is the Son except the Father, nor who is the Father except the son, and whoever the Son wishes to reveal him to.' We read at *J 10:30*, 'I and the Father are one.' These words are fathered on him by his followers, but no doubt his elation was massive, especially since the simple could understand what he was about. There is no doubt but that he projected himself as the divine Wisdom as valid at the End as at the Beginning.[3]

He knew he 'went out' (*Mk 1:38*), and 'was sent' (*L 4:43*), to preach the good news on a royal progress. Nothing should stand in its way (*Mk 2:23–8*). At Capernaum he taught: 'The time [of release] is fulfilled, for the Kingdom of God is near. *Repent* and believe this good news' (*Mt 4:17*). Believe and repent! He alluded to *Is 61:1, 58:6*: preaching the good news to the destitute, freedom to prisoners (of sin), sight to the (spiritually) blind, escape to the (spiritually, not politically) oppressed. This is tantamount to saying that national sins were about to be forgiven (cf. *Ac 5:31*).

Synagogues were his principal stage (*L 4:15; Mt 4:23*), for preaching and healing (cf. *Ps 40:9–10*). Displays of 'spirit-possessed' exhibitionists were terminated. His teaching must have been arresting, and psychologically well founded. If a few believers leavened the lump of society (*Mt 13:13; G 5:9*), audiences would grow (*Mk 1:45*). Since Jesus recommended unloading surplus property in favour

---

1 Babylonian Talmud, *Baba Qamma* 92b; cf. *Judges 4:8*.

2 *Mk 1:41, 9:22; Mt 9:35–6, 15:32, 20:34; L 7:13*.

3 Riesner, *Lehrer*, 329–44 relies on *Mt 11:16–19, 25–6, 28–30, 12:42; J 7:37–8*.

of the destitute he may well have expected the world to reach a consummation in his generation, when accounts would be cast up (*Mt 23:36*). If so, it was on the footing that this consummation was always pending. There was a tone of urgency, so that even those who did not follow him spread the news everywhere (*Mk 10:52; Mt 9:31*). Unpromising patients, healed, did the same (*Mk 1:45, 5:19–20*). No one could bank on avoiding disaster, vigilance was essential, not against war or genocide but hell (*Mt 24:38–43*). The impression received was that anyone who begged his help would be saved (from the Wrath) (*R 10:13, 17*); and faith in him would make a sinner innocent (*R 3:26, 28*), provided faith led to compliance (*J 3:36*).

The Cadres

Some well-placed people asked about his doctrine. His political views were sought (*Mt 22:15–21*); an abstruse question on after-death existence was raised (*23–32*); and common matters of morality (*19:3*). Drawing attention to her accusers' weaknesses he, in effect, rescued a woman about to be stoned for adultery (*J 8:3–11*). One doubts the historicity of the story but it was treasured. Yet, apart from inquisitions (pp. 66–7 above), was his system critically examined? Very few were *asked* to 'follow' him. Yet encouraging factors emerged.

Only in Samaria, which was anti-Jewish, did he experience unreflecting hostility, so as to gag the mission (*L 9:53*), not, however, a substantial rejection of what he offered (*J 4:40*). Elsewhere there was some tolerance, a willingness to take an interest, even curiosity (*L 23:8*). Should he heal foreigners (*Mt 15:23–4*) who had not paid for such privileges (*L 7:5*)? Pharisee 'well-wishers' warned him of King Herod's hostility (*L 13:31*); he seems not to have monitored his image at court. That indefatigable preacher, Paul, would never have preached before notabilities had not the opportunities been thrust on him (*Ac 24:10, 25:23*). A courtier or ex-courtier in the Church, or a female friend at court (*Ac 13:1; L 8:3*) is not really equal to an advocate in high places. The merits of the Word, and therefore of the Way, were not aired in debate except before the High Council in Jerusalem after Jesus' death, where the speakers are flatteringly reported, while the hearers seem not to have applied their minds to the nature of the 'discovery' of which we have been taking notice.

A patient cured by Jesus might well be sincere, and might make himself useful (*Mt 8:15*); but did he understand the doctrine? The small girl can hardly have done so (*Mk 5:41–2*), and one wonders about her distraught parents. One patient was able to defy hostile Pharisees, and 'worshipped' Jesus (*J 9:38*); but he had no idea what Jesus was about. The latter explained to him that his real object was to polarize the population: the 'seeing' would be those who took his unusual view of life, and the 'blind' those who preferred current theology. Indeed, the Man Born Blind, cured in the course of a mime of biblical ideas,[1] was as mystified

1 Derrett at *Evangelical Quarterly* 66 (1994), 251–54.

after his cure as before. And so was the paralytic whose sins were quixotically 'released' (*Mk 2:5*), and another, selected for healing and thereupon abruptly told, 'Sin no more, in order that nothing worse befall you' (*J 5:14*). Can Jesus be said to have convinced him?

Believers were expertly 'fished' by early disciples (*Mk 1:16–20*), who left paying occupations to do this. Some hearers thought they knew enough religion (*L 18:9*), but Jesus did not purport to repair traditional Judaism nor to adapt it (*Mk 2:21–2*). He ridiculed self-righteousness (*L 18:9–14*), an unreliable asset (*R 10:3*). He said nothing less than *rebirth* could make a Christian, and one wondered how (*J 3:3–5*).

If they wanted to be in that flattering group (*1Pe 2:9*), God's 'elect' (*R 16:13; Co 3:12*), they must note that many are called, few chosen (*Mt 22:14*). Who are these, that can influence God's timetable (*Mk 13:20*)? Is intellectual conviction required? At least we are told that saying 'Lord, Lord!' will achieve nothing. This distinct rejection of adulation of himself is very significant. Whereas the desirable kind of assent is never discussed, his want of wholehearted adherence to a mission is fatal (*Mt 8:18–22*). We wonder what depth of guidance was furnished.

Indifferent people could be potentially sympathetic (*Mk 9:40*). But basically the public (as ever) wanted to be esteemed by each other: *God's* estimation of them was too remote to take seriously (*L 16:14–15; J 5:44*), especially in a collective society. Praise or blame from men naturally left Jesus unmoved (*J 5:41*), the genuine ascetical position. Nevertheless, since the first Christians were of varied backgrounds, a method of internal discipline had to be invented. Let wrongdoers confess and repent (*L 17:3*), or the Church will take action (*Mt 18:15–18*). So a category of leader, or supervisor, must emerge. One claimed that the unreliable Peter (of all people) initiated it (*Ac 10:6; 11; 15*). Soon one could protest against individuals domineering over the 'flock' (*1Pe 5:3*).

The core of the movement was those who put money in the purse (*J 12:6*) or provided hospitality (*L 8:3; 1C 9:13*). Patients, healed, were quick enough to serve holy vagrants (*Mt 8:15; J 12:1–2*). Believers' gifts (*G 6:6*) kept the gospel afloat irrespective of synagogues, where its reception could not be predicted.

The Twelve Apostles, able to expel demons and cure diseases and disabilities, were personally selected (*Mt 10:1*) and sent out to preach (*Mk 3:13; L 6:13*). Jesus converted the 'wicked' by personal example (*Mk 2:14–17*); but the apostles, not wasting their efforts (*Mt 7:6*), must be less provocative, wise as serpents and pure as doves (*Mt 10:16*). The Law requires two witnesses to any controversial matter: Jesus' emissaries go off two by two. They seek for 'lost sheep', which does not mean precisely 'wicked'. They proclaim the nearness of the Kingdom, and heal, *gratis* (*Mt 10:5–8*). They take nothing for the road, not even a pouch (*Mk 6:8–11*) – Matthew says not even shoes. They find a house that is 'worthy', enter it with a greeting, and stay there until they move on. Where a village rejects them they are sadly reminded of Sodom and Gomorrha (*Mt 10:15*), which perished because there were not ten good people to be found in them. The Kingdom has come near even those who rejected news of it (*L 10:11*).

The missionaries are like 'sheep' (again) amongst 'wolves' (*Mt 10:16*); they may be flogged to testify (in effect) to their loyalty. The Spirit will coach them in their defence (*L 12:12*): it would be adequate so far as Luke knew (*21:15*); but Paul did not find it so, with all his ability. He expected persecution and recommended his flock to learn how to answer anyone impressively (*Co 4:6*). To be 'acknowledged' by Jesus in the hereafter one must fearlessly admit one's belief in him in this world (*Mt 10:33*). Yet the missionaries' task was shocking, and one can understand why some of them were driven away.

Listeners might fall into factions, even the host family itself (*Mt 10: 34–6*). An idealistic message might attract young hearers and dismay the elders. Did not Jesus foresee that brother would betray brother (to inquisitors from Jerusalem), and children their parents? Early Christians would be hated for Jesus' sake inside Israel and without (*Mt 24:9*). They may be chased from village to village, but the gospel will never be preached to an end (*24:14*). They cannot expect to be treated better than Jesus was (*Mk 13:12–13; Mt 10: 21–5*); at least there is consolation, the authorities cannot send them to hell, they cannot kill their souls (*26–32*). It can be meritorious to be persecuted.

God promises a reward to those who 'receive' missionaries. Are the visitors 'disciples', 'righteous', 'prophets'? The reward corresponds to the status (and therefore the expectations?) of each (*Mk 9:41; Mt 10:40–2*). The hosts' merit is at issue, not their social standing (one hopes). Aftercare is envisaged in favour of converts (*Mt 12:43–5*).

How did Jesus persuade missionaries to encounter a range of dangers without a coin in their belt? The fishermen could fetch up many a useless 'fish' (*Mt 13:47–50*). Jesus is frank: no one is up to his requirements if he loves his home more than Jesus (*Mt 10:37*). *Their* motivation has been tapped, eternal life will be theirs (*Mt 19:29*), and they comply. Satan's wiles are powerless against them (*L 10:17; Ps 91:13*); their names are in the heavenly book (*Ex 32:32–3*). For their 'harvest' many more workers are needed (*Mt 9:37–8*).

Converts funded missionaries into gospel-free regions (*P 4:17; R 12:13*). Categories of 'gifted persons' emerged: prophets were welcomed (*Ac 11:20*); likewise teachers, apostles, and folk speaking in 'kinds of tongues' – the last difficult to use (*1C 14:20*). If there was a hierarchical order (*1C 12:28–30*) these were *designated areas*, and mere workers and helpers were consoled for their gifts' being less dramatic or their risks less appalling. Greater than the gifts were moral endowments. In a famous passage Paul finds that, whereas the 'gifts' were transient, faith, hope, and love were permanent, the greatest being love (*1C 13:1–7*). One can see his point. Teachers and apostles have many compensations and fringe-benefits; and prophets and 'tongues' would be exhibitionists to a man or woman. Paul is clear that self-projection is worth very little if that moral quality, love, is missing.

17

THE PERFECT

THERE were the 'little ones' (*Mk 9:42; 1C 3:1; 1J 2:1*), beginners, with the purity (we hope) of children (*Mt 18:10*), who must grow up in the faith (*H 5:12–14; E 4:14*). Then there were the 'righteous' who had made progress; and lastly the perfect, who had mastered the training. All live in the world, not withdrawn from it (*J 17:15; 1C 5:10*). Occasional sexual activity between spouses was contemplated, or Satan would be given an opening (*1C 7:5*); for unchastity was hated by God (*1T 4:3, 6*) and prostitution abominable (*1C 6:15*). Existence is simplified by celibacy (*1C 7:1*), and missionaries may opt for it, though they may take their wives (at the Church's expense: *1C 9:5, 14*), to avoid involvement with females who might not relish being treated as mothers (*1Ti 5:2*). An attention-seeker preached that Christians should not marry, but he lacked authority (*1Ti 4:3*). Sexual attachments distracted people from being perfect (*1C 7:5, 28*). Since to forswear sex increased performance relative to the Kingdom (*Mt 19:12*), Paul recommended adopting a way of life conducive to 'attendance upon the Lord without distraction' (*1C 7:32–5*). In general he insists that no obligation, real or fancied, should distract one from the constant duty to love one's neighbour as oneself, the total of moral obligation, performance of which could not (at that time) infringe upon any law (*R 13:8–10*), while impurity negates perfection (*2C 7:1*).

The perfect were models. Paul, perfect or not, expected to be imitated (*1C 4:16, 11:1*). They would give up everything to live according to the Good News. Jesus was sad about a likely candidate who could not manage that (*L 18:23*). He was a businessman and his talents would have been helpful. The perfect showed 'mercy' to everyone on the model of God himself (*Mt 5 48; L 6:36*). Clement of Alexandria (after our period) thought the perfect of his day were free from passion, courage, eagerness, anger, desires: but Jesus taught no such thing. The perfect were like the *hasīdīm* of ancient and modern Jewry. They were endlessly forgiving (*Mt 18:23–35*), putting no sense-pleasure before duty; aiming to 'enter into life' (*18:7–10*); showing no resentment, whatever the provocation (*L 9:52–6; R 12:17*); overcoming evil with good (*R 12:21*); making peace by appealing to conscience (*Epistle to Philemon*), and conciliating even slanderers (*1C 4:13*).

It is to the perfect one looks for development of Jesus' all too succinct teaching to meet new problems. Peter, Paul, and no doubt others, developed the Word with confidence (*1C 7:12*). The Word grows by trial and error. One applies the simile of the tree and its fruit: do new rules harmonize with the source?

18

THE FAMILY-MAN'S ETHIC

WITHOUT the householder there would have been no Christianity. He will have noted with satisfaction how acceptable ideas came forward to mitigate the stark visions of the original message: the value of minding one's own affairs, and of work (*1 T 4:11–12; 2T 3:6–12*); of providing for one's relations (*1 Ti 5:8*); the wickedness of idleness (*1 T 5:14; 2T 8:6*); of gossiping (*1 Ti 5:13*); and of free-loading (*1 Ti 5:6*). Tips on how to unload parasites onto charitable individuals (*1 Ti 5:16*) must have been welcome. The Christian, on what some might see as a military operation (*E 6:13–17*), strives as an athlete for an imperishable crown (*1 C 9:25*), a runner (*H 12:1*) who does not want to 'run' (*G 2:2*) with layabouts' baggage on his back. 'Bearing each other's burdens' meant mutual counselling in moral quandaries (*G 6:2*). Deviants must be got rid of (*1 C 5:11*); decency is a general guide (*1 C 14:40*). Offenders can be boycotted (*2T 3:14*), and the Church need not be too tolerant of conceited know-alls, who proliferate in religion (*E 5:25, 6:3*), while mere grumblers are to be admonished (*P 2:14*).

So cheerful givers continued to give (*2C 9:7*), and 'elect ladies' were worth an honourable mention (*2J 1*). Women no doubt overrated their spiritual freedom, and their enthusiasms had to be repressed (*1C 11:5, 14:34;* cf. *1Ti 2:11–12*). Yet they came to Church in finery (*1Ti 2:9*).

Freedom was double-edged. Too much spirit caused disturbances, while not enough of it left the convert a prey to works-righteousness preached energetically by those who thought that Christians must at least look like Jews (*2C 3:6*). Having placed the Law in a situation to be challenged by the spirit, Paul was ready to see all races and statuses as in principle equal, provided their secular (including legal) situation remained unchanged. Householders would not have relished having their slaves (human tools) 'liberated' suddenly.

This was a needful reservation, since the convert had been promised that whatever he gave up would be fully compensated for in the new life and with the new company (*Mk 10:30*), persecution having already been taken into account. He is promised merit if he always chooses the moral high ground, and that he can justify his position (*Mk 13:5–13*). Taking care not to allow *others* to transgress the precepts, he is not to be judgemental, since God recompenses the indulgent (*L 6:37*). Forbearing, forgiving, reconciling, he must also take the initiative in generosity (*L 6:38*), whereas if the Church is Christ's deputy, generosity to it (*Mt 26:2–13*) is highly meritorious. If there was neither Jew nor Greek, slave nor free, male nor female, for all are 'one in Christ Jesus' (*G 3:28*), the chief distinction must lie in expansive generosity, which, of course, would be prestige-building.

Amongst the Ten Commandments (*Ex 20:2–17*) Jesus was interested in 'Kill not', 'Commit no adultery', 'Steal not', 'Give no false witness', 'Honour father and mother'; and he adds, 'Deprive no one of anything', perhaps deriving it from the commandments against stealing, false witness or coveting (*Mk 10:19*). Alas, one can obey all these in the spirit as well as the letter and still be concerned for property and status, missing the goal for which Jesus would have prepared one. This problem is endemic in a deontological system of thought (p. 58). Meanwhile Jesus comported himself not as a philosopher but as a saviour.

The new family promised to believers is not merely a matter of a substituted social network. They have become founder-members of a household of God (*G 6:10; E 2:19; 1Ti 5:8*),[1] a phrase likely to encapsulate both their joy and their pride.

---

1 R.A. Campbell at *NTS* 41/1 (1995), 157–60.

19

HOW THE MESSAGE WAS RECEIVED

As we have seen, it was expected that even families who did receive missionaries would quarrel over their message, while their preaching might bring them into conflict with the synagogue and/or the state. It might even cost them their lives. Paul knew what that meant, having been on both sides of the controversy. The missionaries were not promised an easy passage. Jesus' teaching was *not* commonplace moralizing. Only those whom God had already[1] chosen to learn from Jesus would become believers – an amazingly pessimistic forecast.

His former neighbours at Nazareth were curious enough to attend a sermon of his, but took it as a reflection on themselves (*L 4:25–30*). Celebrated teachers, even miracle-workers, are not expected to be practical;[2] and his knowledge of the Hebrew scriptures must have been prompt and apt (*Mt 12: 5–12*) if he intended to undermine its support for a system of ethics which had proved itself over time. One whose reputation is in part based on exorcisms is open to the accusation that he 'has' a demon, which, if it enables him to drive out other demons, furnishes him with a message likely to seduce Israel into apostasy. Suggestions that he was mad (*Mk 3:20–1; J 10:20; 2C 5:13*) and the like (*J 8:49, 52*) are not entirely met by the claim that he was the light of the world (*J 9:5*), one claim made for him (*J 1:9*), or that he was sinless (*J 8:46;* cf. *9:24*), and a prophet (*9:17*). One can be a false prophet, whose self-praise is meaningless (*8:13*). Resistance was lively.

In the parable of the Great Supper (*L 14:15–24*) people who had been invited sent excuses and failed to come. The excuses were plausible enough; each expected not to be missed. No one came. Naturally worldly concerns make an invitation to a banquet in the next world uninviting – the chance can wait. No one will expect to be struck off the guest-list. The parable of the Wicked Tenants of the Vineyard was aimed at the minority governing Israel (*Mt 21:33–45*). Jesus' message would be weak wherever social pressure, convenience, or profit stood in its way. One may have ears to hear with and still not 'hear' (*Mk 8:18;* cf. *11:15, 13:16*), a NT cliché. His survival of crucifixion made a difference. But it added nothing to his precepts or their clarity, and the character of primitive Christianity was almost settled in his lifetime.

---

1 *J 6:44; R 8:28–9; E 1:4.* There is no suggestion that they had been ultra-pious in previous lives. The idea is not explained.

2 Plutarch, *Moralia* 43F.

VERMEER (1632–75) *Christ in the House of Martha and Mary*
National Gallery of Scotland, Edinburgh
Bridgeman Art Library, London

DUCCIO (1260–C. 1318). *Jesus appoints the eleven as teachers* (Matthew 28:19–20)
Siena, Museo dell'Opera Metropolitana

Scala, Firenze

Jewish Tolerance

Ascetic groups within Israel (p. 63) did not suffer at the hands of the hierarchy at Jerusalem, however negative the latter might be towards religious enthusiasm. Judaism was a broad religious denomination, with its few unmistakable landmarks, viz. the descent from Abraham, circumcision, the escape from Egypt, Passover, the covenant with Yahweh at Sinai, the Sabbath rest, the Babylonian Exile. If a Jew did not abuse the Temple cult, or Moses, or participate in an idolatrous cult (note *1C 8*) he was in little danger, whatever his theories or his mysteries, if any.

From the New Testament we gather that intolerance was shown towards Jesus' programme, and, after his time, towards his followers. This was not simply because of claims that he was Son of God, the alleged Messiah, or of his reappearance after crucifixion. What was more threatening to the government at Jerusalem was his doctrine. Against him there stood the Law and the Prophets and the whole of civilized society symbolized by the Pharisees and the rest, by Herod, and by Rome. There being no written constitution for the Jewish state, scripture had to do duty for one, and that meant interpretation. It had been interpreted so as to maintain a balance between the demands of Yahweh and the capacities of Jews. Jesus now taught his followers to turn the other cheek, and to love enemies, not to turn away from anyone wanting to borrow, etc., and he was some sort of mystic who performed miracles and acquired a following. Caesar must be obeyed (he claimed) so as not to diminish the rights of God. If not revolutionary, this was at least threatening.

From the gospels we can tell that the populace who had nothing to lose were with Jesus in any controversy he might have with the priesthood, the arch-collaborators with Rome. The people were enthusiastic (*L 19:48*) and must have been thrilled to hear that Jesus foretold that the scribes would go to hell for dishonestly handling widows' estates (*Mk 12:40*).

Did his Cleansing of the Temple influence official attitudes towards his movement? He threw merchants out of it, overturning the tables of the money-changers and the seats of dove-sellers, claiming (after *Is 56:7*) that that 'house' was to be a house of prayer, whereas (*Jr 7:11*) they had made it a den of robbers (*Mt 21:12–13*). He had an opinion of that grandiose structure (*Mk 13:1–2*) consistent with his doctrine, viz. that relations with God are established by intention and conduct, not architecture. Judged by that criterion, the worship of God had become a commercial enterprise; for the priests were directly and/or indirectly profiting from the Law relating to offerings. This is 'robbery' judged by a criterion cropping up again at *R 2:17–24*, where Paul asks friends at Rome whether they are not guilty of sins for want of enough scruples. Since the priests had a bad reputation, Jesus was justified in miming a search of a suspect house for leprosy (*Lv 14:33–53*).[1] To claim he was engineering a revolution is otiose. On the other hand

---

1 Derrett at *SNT* 5: 96–113.

one would have to be exceptionally tolerant to condone such violent behaviour even granted there might appear to be some excuse for it. A superstitious people would be agog. The Cleansing of the Temple is an instance of Jesus' methods, but hardly a sufficient ground for concocting a case against him before the Roman governor.

Analysing what happened, Luke saw Jesus as a catalyst who caused the negligent to 'fall' and the pious to 'rise'; he symbolized contradictions (with established ideas) and distressing dissensions (*L 12:51–3*); his mother would suffer from their parting (*L 2:35*); while his challenge to Israel exposed the indirect motives of many (*L 2:34–5*). He claimed that as the Kingdom was dawning it was an abuse that doors should be shut against entrants (*L 16:16*) by men who do not intend to enter themselves (*Mt 23:13*). Merit-free entrants, i.e. whores and taxgatherers and their like (*Mt 21:31–2*), were privileged in this regard. All that they had to do was to respond.

Pharisees took away the key of knowledge (to keep for themselves: *L 11:52*), while Jesus had given the keys of the Kingdom to a fisherman, Peter (*Mt 16:19*)! There everyone is of higher status even than John the Baptist, who was Elijah in another guise (*Mt 11:11, 14*). Jesus' teaching comes from God (*J 7:16–17*) and therefore he does what he likes on the Sabbath (*Mk 3:6*), a direct threat to good order. Jesus' opponents are children of the devil (*J 8: 44*); they will die in their sins (*8:21, 24*). The patriarchs anticipated him (*56*). Pharisees were 'blind guides' (*Mt 23:16–22, 24*), 'unmarked tombs' by which the incautious could be defiled (*L 11:44*). Their proselytes were children of hell (*Mt 23:15*). He did not doubt he would be slandered in turn (*Mt 5:11*).

He precipitated debate about himself (*J 7:12–13, 32, 40–3*), which continues. The populace who approved of him cannot have seen his doctrine as being all gloom and self-denial. The precept, 'If anyone wishes to follow me, let him deny himself, take up his cross, and follow me', requires self-humiliation in penitence (cf. *Job 42:6*) and in renunciation of normal ambitions, taking any risk in joining the mission. It does not refer to any theory of the self, and it cannot be confined to kamikaze missionaries. Believers should save their souls rather than gain the whole world. There must have been optimists who welcomed this saying or it would not have been preserved, likewise the optimistic idea that the weary activist would find 'rest' (*Mt 11:28–9*, cf. *Ex 33:14*).

The Package
The stark negative aspects in his teaching have to be balanced by consequential positive aspects. A personality cleared of aggression must be an asset – no one suggests that the ideal was total passivity. The Kingdom was likened to a treasure or an exquisite pearl (*Mt 13:44–6*), obviously a lucrative package. Were the profits realizable only in the next world, an uncashable cheque?

Paul saw this point, though not acutely. The next generations believed the Christian virtues needed to be listed. A mini-code of virtue exists (*Titus*). One avoids evil and practises good (*J 5:29; 1Pe 3:11; 3J 11*), a combination bound to be widely welcomed. The list of vices at *Mt 15:19* is conventional, since the Old Testament has similar ones (*Jr 7:9; Ps 53:1–3; Ho 4:2–3*).

The family man heard what he expected to hear. 'Virtue' is not a stock New Testament word, but we hear of long-suffering (a favourite NT term), goodness, generosity (*G 5:22–3*); simplicity; self-control (*Ac 24:25; 1C 7:9, 9:25*), gratitude (a favourite word with Paul); mercifulness and pity (*1 Pe 3:8*); readiness to bear oppression (*2C 11:20*); humility (*P 2:3*), a prime virtue in Jesus' eyes; mutual obligingness (*E 4:32*); peaceableness (*Jas 3:17–18*) and mildness; sobriety and decency (*1Ti 2:9, 15*); and lastly joy, another favourite word of Paul's. It is possible to see behind the terms something similar to the outstanding Greek virtues, 'philanthropy' and 'piety'.

Such a picture of the new society would attract many recruits amongst Jews. At *L 18:11* we see a Pharisee congratulating himself on not being like the generality of people who are rapacious, unjust, and adulterous. *Ps 34:12–16* contains a code of good behaviour: no evil speaking, no guile, avoiding evil, doing good, seeking peace, for God's anger against evildoers eliminates even the memory of them: *1Pe 2:1* takes all this up. There is a marvellous list of virtues at *2Pe 1:5–7*. Christianity expected every commonplace virtue of its members. At *E 4:30–2* it is said to be painful to God that the 'sealed' (i.e. baptized) should show any bitterness, passion, anger, brawling, slander, since they must be mutually generous, tender-hearted, forgiving as God forgave them through Christ. Paul urges his converts to control their speech, a long-lasting problem. A fine exhortation occurs at *P 4:8*: 'Whatever is true, honourable, just, pure, lovely, gracious, any excellence, or anything worthy of praise, fix your mind on these.' By inference the Greek vice, *hybris* (insolent cruelty), was ruled out without referring to it. One could hardly complain of such folk, or of such as hold the following to be vices:

> Evil designing (*Mt 15:19*); sinning (a characteristic of the heathen: *Mk 14:41*); injustice; depravity; fornication, uncleanness; theft, murder (*1Ti 1:9*); anger, enmity; faction (a recurrent problem), hatred (*1J 2:9*); envy (*R 1:29*); adultery; idolatry; covetousness; sensuality (*G 5:19, 21*); homosexuality (*1C 6:9*); rapacity; avarice; stinginess (*Mk 7:22*); jealousy; roguery; guile, unseemly behaviour; abuse and slander; selfish ambition; treacherousness; lying (*Co 3:9; 1Ti 1:10*); false witness; pride, folly (*Mk 7:22*); poisoning; disobedience; singularity of opinion(!) (*G 5:20–1*); unbelief; drunkenness; foolish talk; and instability.

Sinners will not 'inherit' the Kingdom (*1C 6:9–10*), for the works of the 'flesh' (*G 5:19–20*) are foreign to Christians. Alas, even in Paul's time converts were still being 'fleshly' (*1C 3:3*).

The generations after Jesus have not been loud in recommending love of the enemy, or doing to others as one would wish them to do to oneself. One is told, in doubt, to reflect what conduct would please the Lord (*E 5:10*), not deserting common sense (*1C 10:14*).

Refusal to be Persuaded

Cultural differences explained many disagreements with Christian propagandists (*Ac 28:24–8*). A rich man, however, understanding Jesus' requirement about coveting, refused to sell all he had and give the proceeds to the poor (*L 18:23*). He had always obeyed a selection of the Ten Commandments (the tenth, not to covet, is not listed), but this was buying perfection at too high a price. He was not fleshly-minded (*P 3:19*), simply cautious.

Jesus' generation was, however perversely, disinclined to join in his project (*Mt 11: 16–19*), and in his lifetime he was not merely rejected (he did not pass the world's test) but also made to suffer for it (*L 17:25*). He complained that cities which knew his miracles would not repent: his own loyalty proved their wickedness (*Mt 11:20–4*). Controversialists challenged him to convince them by a miracle, but he declined (*Mt 12:39;* cf. *J 6:30–1*). The spiritual leaders of his day were, he said, hypocrites (*Mt 15:7*); but there is no evidence that *hasīdīm* disapproved of him. Something obstructed the Jews' attention to the Word (*J 8:43–4*); it impressed the multitude but no one in power accepted it (*J 7:46–7*). Jesus' own brothers were not only sceptical of his enterprise, prior (that is) to the Resurrection (which altered their own prospects), but even sarcastic about it. Opposition was widespread (*Mt 28:17b; L 2:34; Ac 19:25–7; 1C 1:23–4*).

Perhaps his words were spirit and life, and the flesh was useless without them – but belief is hindered by unseen factors (*J 6:63–5*). It may be culpable blindness not to react conformably to his proclamation (*J 9:39, 41*); but the fact remains that only a minority would subscribe to it, despite attempts to promote his mission as a variety of Jewish piety – for the world's hostility was a permanent obstacle (*1J 3:1*).

20

THE COST

So far the tale has been woeful. Committed Christians have to be exhorted by Paul and his successors to show ordinary virtues which even pagans took for granted. The friction Jesus created, and in turn endured, can be regarded as an 'input', but to what did the 'output' amount – a group having a strange morality? One wonders at his temerity. But is not this the fate of many innovators? As he read scripture and life on the ground the time was ripe for the Kingdom to come soon (*L 18:8*). He had only to make the proclamation and leave the rest to the Word's power of growth. Yet this was too speculative. A centurion might have boundless faith in Jesus' ability to cure his 'boy' (*L 7:7*); but could that centurion advance Jesus' cause with Jewish opponents? Jesus' option was as bizarre as his message. He saw himself as a redeemer of 'many' (*Mk 10:45*), but the cost has been heavy.

Who will be reassured to be told that the flogging of Christians and their persecution by the hierarchy was prophesied by Jesus as a natural sequel to the murder of innocents from time immemorial (*Mt 23:34–6*; cf. *Jr 7:25–6*)? By the time of the Fourth Gospel to confess Jesus as the Messiah was to court boycott from Jewish society (*J 9:22*), for Jesus' death could be considered an advantage to the public (*J 11:47–8*). Hindsight or not, it is made plausible by the narrative of his trial and crucifixion. He misled[1] the people into unpredictable behaviour in the guise of Jewish piety and to eliminate his group would be beneficial. Jews even as far away as Damascus could be subject to violent treatment for taking seriously the Way Jesus had preached (*Ac 9:2*).

By the time of *Revelation* (AD 80?) Christians had been executed for the testimony they had given to their faith in Christ, behaviour unacceptable to the state. Paul himself had been roughly treated (*2C 11:24*). Martyrdom was an established idea by *Hebrews*, *1 Timothy* and *1 Clement*, all works of post-Pauline piety. There must have been many individuals whom Jesus had fatally persuaded to persevere. But seeds of decay were present from the first in spite of the invocation of martyrs' memories.

Vicarious Merit and Corruption
The objections to the new faith were most probably based on convention and caution, but even where it established itself it was subject to weaknesses for which

1 Derrett at *Bijdragen* 55 (1994), 43–55 = *SNT* 6:202–14.

85

Jesus could not be blamed. For example, it was believed to be meritorious to maintain missionaries (*Mt 10:11*) (p. 76 above). Honour given to Jesus created a perpetual credit (*Mt 26:13*). The idea was vigorously canvassed (*1C 16:15–18; P 4:17; 3J 5–8*); and to support counter-preachers, heretics, was sinful, not merely non-meritorious (*2J 11*). One might argue whether it was more meritorious to feed preachers or to listen to them (*L 10:42*)! Such a quandary shows how deeply vicarious merit was entrenched. One could undergo baptism for the sake of transferring the merit to the dead (*1C 15:29*).

Substituting things for people is an analogous superstition. Touching Jesus' garment conveys healing (*Mt 9:20*), for 'power went out of him' (*L 6:19*). Contact with a preacher's body indirectly will heal (*Mk 6:56; Ac 19:12*), also a preacher's shadow (*Ac 5:15*). Such primitive ideas undermine the precept to avoid evil and do good. It is easier to feed a holy man than to comprehend his message, and still easier than to practise it.

Jesus himself is sarcastic at the expense of those who used his name to teach or heal without personal merit (*Mt 7:23*), and even of those who ate with him (cf. *Ex 24:11*) and listened to his sermons. Even such quasi-patronage will not save them from a cutting remark on the Last Day, 'Who are you? Be off, wicked people [*Ps 6:9*]!' Jesus has no time for vicarious merit (on *Mt 25:1–12 see* above p. 70). He has not been listened to: the unhappy theory built cathedrals and monasteries, and is vigorous in Judaism still.

Reform of ideas was retarded by the theory of the Crucifixion, which turned his execution under the orders of Pilate, the governor, into a gift. The giving of his life for 'many' (*Mk 10:45*) would make no sense, in spite of its model at *Is 53:4, 10–11*, if his sufferings were not adopted by others in payment for their 'debts'. Paul preaches this doctrine as axiomatic (*R 4:25*). Jesus took upon himself the woes and sins of others (*Is 53*), as claimed at *Mt 8:7*. His merit was transferable. Paul says, 'While we were sinners Christ died for us' (*R 5:8*): the unmeritorious gain merit through another's obedience to the cross (*P 2:8*). But though this supports the objectionable idea of vicarious merit, it is an open question whether Jesus himself somehow authorized it.

How far could he foresee that he would suffer death, and that others, his 'friends', would be advantaged thereby, irrespective of any merit on their own parts? The answer may lie in the theory of 'handing over'. If God handed over his disobedient people to the enemy as punishment, Jews who adopted Jesus' being 'handed over' to the Romans as an advantageous transaction would be relying on the principle of ethnic solidarity, and this was never an object of sarcasm on Jesus' part.

Many think his predictions (*Mk 8:31*) that he would suffer severely for his enterprise were 'prophecies after the event'. But there was a near-precedent for his situation, which did not receive the dramatization accorded to the Crucifixion. The Spartans, as is notorious, were a people who consistently achieved greatness with no resources save their magnificent discipline and ability to sacrifice individuality to the common good. After laxity had crept in, young Agis, king of Sparta (244–1 BC), attempted an idealistic reform in the direction of tightening discipline. His scheme came to nothing due to treachery or corruption.[1] The Spartans were only human, after all. He was assassinated; he had failed to persuade a sufficient number of rich and poor to accept a regime of traditional austerity with the object of securing Sparta's survival. But the reforms, in another guise, were carried out by King Cleomenes about fourteen years later. Jesus' scheme was further-reaching than Agis', and, despite his miracles, it was only a matter of time before a powerful attempt would be made to stifle it. Men wanted to avoid hell, but without commotion or a process of social 'winnowing' (*Mt 3:12*).

Because of the theory of vicarious merit it was scarcely necessary to be meritorious oneself, provided one believed in the sacrifice of Christ. Paul's clear denials of this (*1C 6:8–11; G 5:16–26;* cf. *E 5:1–14*) were overlooked. As soon as the Church became a treasury not merely of merit but also of cash made available for charitable purposes, headship of it became a marketable commodity. A form of electioneering, bursts of doctrinal novelty (*2J 7*), and manipulation of factions and schisms, all were tried,[2] due, it was said, to greed and love of money (*1Ti 6:3–10*). The quarrels were not about doctrine but who should handle the loaves and fishes (*P 3:19; 1Ti 3:8*). Schismatics carouse with their cronies (*2Pe 2*). *The First Epistle of Clement* (AD 96–8) attempts to reverse a local decision at Corinth to dismiss their bishop: the merit of the quarrel is ignored in favour of subordination.

One has been able to make a fortune in any way and with it build a synagogue or a church, consecrating one's name in the odour of sanctity. One's pride may allow one to open one's hand to the poor. The rich rely on litigation, though that was condemned by Jesus and Paul (*1C 6:1–8*). The *Epistle of James* claims rich members of the Church made themselves objectionable. 'Whosoever would be a friend of the world makes himself an enemy of God.' It seems the Church fell into factions which did not resist the devil (*4:7*). The Tempter is the god of this world (*2C 4:4*); he could attack even Peter (*L 22:31*) and enter into Judas (*J 13:27*). He must be watched for (*2C 2:11*), because of his disguises (*11:14*). He is ubiquitous and one cannot be sufficiently alert (*1Ti 5:15; 1Pe 5:8*). Sound doctrine has no time for undisciplined, irreligious, sinful, unholy and profane people; but the Church has plenty of them (*1Ti 1:9*). Jesus' picture of the steward who, when his master was away, beat his fellow-servants and drank himself stupid (*Mt 24:45–51*) was an accurate forecast. The returning master will remind him of hell; for one must be faithful in 'little things'. But when will Christ come again?

1 Plutarch, *Agis* 8, 1–2.

2 *1J 2:19; 2J 9–11; 3J 9–10; Jude 4, 8.*

We are in the Last Days (*1J 2:18*), must live soberly (*R 12:3*) and not be subject to desires (*R 13:13–14*). This is just the period when vices, and love of pleasure, rather than God, will make Christians like pagans (*2Ti 3:2–5; R 1:29–32*). Those that defy God deserve death, and those too who approve of their doings (*R 1:32*). Love will get cold, said Matthew (*24:10–14*). Too true. If Jesus taught a norm recognizable by rabbis[1] its effect was short-lived. But there is more.

Treachery

Apart from their generally dismal tone, the first three gospels insist that Jesus foretold he would be handed over to gentiles, to face a shameful death. All gospels show him going willingly to his death, though he does not specifically instruct any of his party to betray him. 'Handing over' is one thing, 'betrayal' is another. The gospels contrive to make the first, which post-Resurrection theology adopted (*see* above p. 86), look like the latter.

The story has no cheerful aspect. The closest disciples were incompetent in general (*Mk 9:32,* a comment repeated *six* times), they could not protect him (*Mt 26:22*), or even influence him in his own interest (*Mt 16:22–3; J 11:8*). There is a contrast between Peter's boastfulness (*Mt 26:35*) and the general desertion of Jesus at his 'capture' at Gethsemane. 'All fled.' Their weakness is not deplored; their sleepiness, yes (*Mk 14:37*). At the Last Supper Judas Iscariot is identified as the traitor (*Mt 26:23*); it could have been any of the Twelve (*26:22*). The one who begrudged waste, and did not think of the poor (*J 12:6*), the thief, does the betraying. One of the Twelve *had* to do it (*Mt 26:14–16*), no doubt in hindsight.

After the Resurrection Paul acted as a zealous persecutor of Christians (*Ac 8:3*), who were constantly afraid of betrayal (*Ac 12:16–17*). People of little courage survived to tell the tale: that must be the point of this story.

Though corruption became endemic in the Church, and weak individuals obtained leadership positions, often successfully, the Word continued to be preached. Leaders began to quarrel (*3J 9–11*); the virtues of patience, forbearance and mutual deference were overlooked. Paul recommended that fornicators, frauds and idolaters should be boycotted (*1C 5:10–11*). He could have saved his ink: they could pay for company that was not fussy. The Church spread, a marvel, the surest proof of the appeal of Jesus' teaching.[2] It continues to impress even those who have no intention of obeying it.

---

1 Phillip Sigal, *The Halakhah of Jesus of Nazareth according to the Gospel of Matthew* (Lanham, MD: University Press of America, 1986).

2 Giovanni Boccaccio, *Decameron* (1348), First Day, novel 2 (Abraham, a Jew…).

21

CHRISTIANITY

WITH its sombre auspices one wonders how the new faith survived. But there is more. Let vicarious merit be a deleterious doctrine, the worship of Jesus as God must be an even more inopportune development. Divine attributes attached to him (*Co 1:19, 2:9*), and it was believed forgiveness might be obtained from God through him. That Jews already thought of Wisdom, Power and the Word as emanations from the deity excuses but does not remove this anomaly. Jesus' words at *J 8:31–6* are instructive: 'If you remain in my Word you are truly my disciples, and will know the truth, and the truth will free you. Every sinner is a slave to sin…If the son [i.e. himself] frees you you will really be free.' Jesus is intelligible as an *agent* for God, but as an aspect of God he is a problem, even as the embodiment of Wisdom (*see* above pp. 73, 103). The apostate emperor Julian ridiculed Jesus for offering baptism to seducers and murderers and forgiveness to any who repented,[1] and this objection remains valid. The promise of God's acceptance is an assurance of a very cheap grace, for no self-sacrificial love is prescribed.[2]

The candidate for healing prostrates himself before Jesus according to the gospels (*Mt 8:2: Mk 1:40; L 5:12*). A 'servant' of Jesus will be honoured by God (*J 12:26*). One thinks of his (very special) burial and offers worship (*12:7*). John brings Jesus as close to God as he can without infringing upon Jewish monotheism.[3] To Paul Jesus is a surrogate for the deity (*P 2:6–11; 1C 1:24*). As I have already indicated, angels figured in Jewish mythology; they appear frequently in the New Testament, and Jesus is more than the angels (*H 1:4–5*), and more important than the Temple (*Mt 12:6*). No wonder it was reported that his enemies supposed he made himself out to be God (*J 10:33*). Elation, however understandable, must have limits; yet if Jesus was successful no hyperbole was unthinkable. Did he himself connive at this development?

A woman sought to flatter him by praising his mother (perhaps a polite remark).[4] He reproved her: only those are 'blessed' who hear the Word of God and keep it - a neat pun (*L 11:28*). This is not heeded, and praise of and thanksgiving

---

1 Julian, *Caesars* 336A–B (Loeb edn., II 412–13).

2 Gustafson, *Theology and Ethics* (1981), 18–20.

3 *J 8:38, 10:30, 14:9, 16:28.*

4 Cf. Xenophon, *Hellenica* 4.4, 19; Euripides, *Hypsipyle,* 4 (at D.L. Page, ed., *Select Papyri* III [Loeb edn., 82].

to Jesus take the place of obedience. The 'output' is so easily gained that the minimum of 'input' seems to suffice. The observance of fasting which is easier than loving one another (*J 13:35*) and certainly than loving one's neighbour, was maintained even though Jesus thought his followers should celebrate the joy of salvation.

Fortunately a living spirit which took Jesus' place after his departure from the scene had enough initiative to enable Christianity to emerge as an intercultural cult (*Ac 15:19–20, 28–9*). But this sanctifies human ingenuity in fact; and dignity was given to a group of as few as two or three provided they believed they acted as Jesus' assessors (*Mt 18:19–20*). This, coupled with the concept of Jesus as divine, exalts the management. The deification of Jesus lends stature to the successors of Judas, and that was perhaps its true origin. Deification does nothing for the one deified, but much for the deifiers (*see* p. 12).[1]

Throughout the ages there have been Christians who attempted to live according to the gospel, so far as they could understand it. Simultaneously it has served as an income for 'shepherds' whose 'shepherding' has been either inadequate or counter-productive, as is notorious. It could be argued that not to know what was required of the baptized takes us back to the time when Peter had to have a dream upon a roof in order to cancel dietary laws. The reformed churches of the sixteenth century attempted to go into this problem, to go back to the texts and to take them seriously.

Even after a century of polemic and bible-study it was easier for clergy to preach about anything but the Lord's prayer and the Ten Commandments. An illiterate parishioner, father of an illegitimate child, could seriously defend himself on the ground that though he had attended church every Sunday for seven years he never heard the minister read out 'Thou shalt not commit adultery'. He commented, 'Probably had you told me my duty, I had not committed this folly!'[2]

It could be claimed as a stroke of genius for Jesus not to specify unmistakably what 'following him' meant. To codify the so-called Commandments of Yahweh in the age of the Jewish Sages, and to teach them, till all 613 have been mastered (including many which are nowhere in use), is a great work. But no one has done this for Christianity, though scope for transition and development was provided (*Mt 18:18–20*), if not by Christ himself at least shortly after his time. On the other hand something can be deduced from those of the Ten Commandments which he cited, much from common sense, and much from his successors as teachers. The somewhat meagre and unoriginal directions at *E 4–5*, and the pru–dent advice given to husbands and wives, parents and children, slaves and their masters, are so common-sensical that we do not need to repeat them (*E 5–6*). They do not serve to link Jesus' principal precepts with everyday problems; but attempts have been made to do this, with some success. A commentary can be

---

1 The deification of Roman emperors is known to have been a means whereby the status of freedmen and even slaves (as priests) was enhanced.

2 Thomas Fuller, *Mixt Contemplations in Better Times* (London, 1660), pt. 2, xlv.

appended to each of the Ten Commandments[1] with every word verified from the bible itself. This method was adopted in the *Larger Catechism* (1648) of the Church of Scotland, which is awesome in its comprehensiveness. It suffices to take two examples:

Questions 138–9:

Q. 138. What are the *duties required* in the seventh commandment?

A. The duties...are chastity in body, mind, affections, words, and behaviour; and the preservation of it in ourselves and others; watchfulness over the eyes and all the senses; temperance, keeping of chaste company, modesty in apparel; marriage by those that have not the gift of continency; conjugal love and cohabitation; diligent labour in our callings; shunning all occasions of uncleanness, and resisting temptations to it.

Q. 139. What are the *sins forbidden* in the seventh commandment?

A. The sins forbidden...besides the neglect of the duties required, are adultery, fornication, rape, incest, sodomy, and all unnatural lusts; all unclean imaginations, thoughts, purposes, and affections; all corrupt or filthy communications, or listening thereunto; wanton looks, impudent or light behaviour, immodest apparel; prohibiting of lawful or dispensing with [i.e. authorizing] unlawful marriages; allowing, tolerating, keeping of brothels, or resorting to them; entangling vows of single life; undue delay of marriage; having more wives or husbands than one at the same time; unjust divorce, or desertion; idleness, gluttony, drunkenness, unchaste company; lascivious songs, books, pictures, dancings, stage plays; and all other provocations to, or acts of, uncleanness, either in ourselves or others.

If one accepts this religion, modern entertainments and their industries are barred to one. When the English public cast off in 1660 the 'Puritan' supervision exercised over them for some years by a Presbyterian ministry, one can imagine the general joy. And yet every precept is reasonably to be derived from the biblical texts; and, of course, they have a further, 'unseen', purpose not evident on the surface of the words. We shall come to this presently.

Meanwhile I find in the Rules of the United Society of Wesleyan Methodists promulgated by John and Charles Wesley in 1743 a requirement of those who seek admission to a Society or to continue in it. It vaguely reminds me of the *Pātimokkha* (*see* p. 44). Those who seek to join must declare 'a desire to flee from the wrath to come [*Mt 3:7*], to be saved from their sins [*R 5:9*]'. Further, they may continue so long as they *firstly* avoid sin, and *secondly* do good (*R 2:9–10*). Doing evil is specified as including:

Taking the Name of God in vain or profaning the Sabbath; drunkenness, or buying, selling or even drinking liquor; brawling, fighting, litigating; using many words in

---

1 Thomas Watson (d. 1686), *The Ten Commandments* (London: Banner of Truth, 1959). This work appears to have been vol. 3 of *A Body of Practical Divinity*, which went into various editions.

buying or selling; dealing in smuggled goods; usury; uncharitable conversation; doing to others as we would not they should do to us; doing what is not for the glory of God, e.g. costly clothing; profane amusements (diversions); singing or reading not tending to the knowledge of God; self-indulgence; laying up treasure on earth; irresponsible borrowing or taking goods on credit.

Doing good is illustrated in a much shorter list:

Doing good, being merciful to people; feeding them; clothing them; visiting the sick or prisoners [*Mt 25:36*]; instructing, reproving, exhorting them in need of it; helping one another *and possible recruits*, e.g. in business; being diligent and frugal for the honour of the gospel; denying themselves, taking up the cross daily [*L 9:23*]; submitting to reproaches, and accepting abuse and contempt with equanimity.

Further they must attend the exercises of their faith participating in the cult and study of scripture: all of which is reasonable seeing the weight which these rules place upon the member. Those that fail would be admonished: 'If he repent not he has no more place with us.'

The reverend authors end with the significant words, 'We have delivered our own souls.' This is a quotation from *Ez 3:19, 21*, repeated at *33:9*, itself alluded to by the author of *1 Ti 4:16*. Whether the members of the Society come up to scratch or not the leaders of the movement are safe in their consciences if they have done all they could to warn, reprove, and exhort, so that every member should 'escape the wrath to come'.

By 1827 the priest-poet John Keble was able to write (the emphasis is mine):

> The trivial round, the common task,
> Will furnish all we ought to ask –
> Room to *deny ourselves*, a road
> To bring us, daily, nearer God.

Now, however, the proclamation of Christ's Resurrection and God's forgiveness tends to take the place of moral guidance and the confidence of meriting the divine favour (*see* p. 126). Christianity, in general, has become a religion without striving: Jesus' impact on his own generation is not reproduced. Sympathy will be felt for modern comments:

To paint sin in its genuine colours, to denounce the wrath of God...this is pharisaical punctiliousness, intolerable rigour, illiberal superstition, the frenzy of bigotry, the bitterness of misanthropy: the sons of *candour* and *charity* turn away with contempt.

For after all at that period preachers were entertainers and paid as such.[1] A modern comment may be accepted:

---

1 I was made aware of Thomas Gisborne (d. 1846) and his *Sermons* (many editions), and therefore of this piece of satire, by Prof. James M. Gustafson.

It was once thought the proper pattern for the Christian was of honesty in business, diligence, good-natured concern for others, stable family life, regularity in church attendance, avoidance of ostentation, giving to good causes. Extremes would be avoided. But now the pattern of life in affluent countries looks almost blasphemous. The character of the culture becomes more and more shallow, superficial and rootless. Its values look absurd, and its status symbols ever more tawdry.[1]

Apart from communities like the Isle of Lewis (in the Hebrides), and the Old Order Amish (in the USA), one wonders where the primitive faith reigns. And yet the West is considered Christian and innumerable works of exhortation pour from the presses, though in an encyclopedia article about Jesus his teaching occupies a derisory space.[2] Meanwhile the corruptions of 'Christian' territories are too manifold to list.

---

1 Cf. Richard G. Jones, *Groundwork of Christian Ethics* (London: Epworth, 1984), 209–10.

2 B.M. Metzger and M.D. Coogan, edd., *Oxford Companion to the Bible* (New York & Oxford: Oxford University Press, 1993), 356–66 (1½ out of 20½ columns).

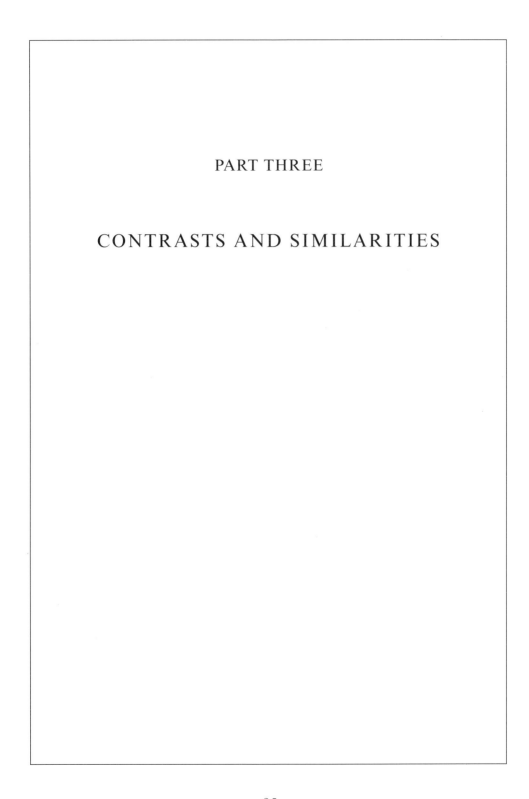

PART THREE

CONTRASTS AND SIMILARITIES

22

ENVIRONMENTS AND BACKGROUNDS

THOUGH both backgrounds, Buddhist and Christian, were collective societies, and the style of teaching in each case was *preceptive*, it remains true that the Buddha's teaching arose in a region where it was accepted (with whatever regrets) that the individual was the ultimate judge of what was right and wrong for himself. His caste, his tribe, his family, his land with its mixture of races and traditions would shape what was *expected* of him, and a group of roles added up to a person who owed (so he would think) loyalty to many others. But simply because of those conflicts, which many found unbearable, or bearable only conditionally, the individual needed to determine what he must do in every dilemma, and what was his ultimate duty. No gods, no ancestors, no sages determined it for him. He could escape into an endless variety of 'vows' or 'renunciation'. A renunciate might prescribe a solution to him, but from that too he might need to escape. The package offered to him would be teleologically conceived.

Consequently an ethical system would appeal to him which assumed that he could secure his *unseen* as well as *seen* (i.e. ostensible) welfare while he went through the many motions of securing others' welfare. Many a wife, and more widows, must have avoided suicide only because Gotama's double-edged answer (*see* p. 33) was available. The extravagant joy surrounding the image of the Buddha shows how valuable his technique must have been.

In Palestine in the time of Jesus once again society had its claims on loyalty, but these were presented to the mind as if they were obligations to Yahweh, the deity whom the Jew believed was not merely superior to other gods, but the only God. Deontological in character, the system depended from Yahweh's supposed will. And that was most variously interpreted by people whose interests in the truth were obscure. The individual found himself the target for teaching, and Wisdom writers addressed him as 'My son'. Whatever the limitations implied by his place in the order of things, he would decide how he would comport himself. Society's ability to force him was restricted. He could not escape responsibility by citing superior orders.

Whereas the Buddha's teaching developed with a seeming logic out of presuppositions drawn from observation and the conventional hypotheses (about the cycle of birth and rebirth), the teaching of Jesus proceeded on the basis that Yahweh's demands for self-control and respect for others' needs took priority (subject to the Golden Rule) over worldly advantages and contrivances of a short-term character. Whereas the Buddha wanted X to be kind to Y for X's sake, Jesus wanted X to be kind to Y for God's sake and therefore for X's sake.

Both Palestine and Northern India knew a number of competing ethical systems, and therefore conflicting prescriptions for successful behaviour. The Buddha's gained prominence in Indian cultural areas because it was a Middle Way; Jesus' for a while in Palestine not because it made moderate demands (the 'light yoke' idea) but because its ultra-pious and ascetic quality made every other system seem by contrast hypocritical and disloyal to God.

The long parable of the Unmerciful Servant (*Mt 18:23–34*) could not have been framed in a Buddhist environment because it is theistic and relies on a God whose demands are overriding. The servant who thought more of his own situation than the needs of another servant of the same master jeopardized the master's interests and thereby disobeyed him, though the latter was a model of generosity (*L 7:42–3*). The lesson is not quite impossible in Buddhist terms: one who has the chance of becoming a *buddha* should not rest content with that, until he has performed a vow to bring others with him to the blissful state. Needless to say, the theory of Christ's own sacrifice would find an echo in a Mahāyāna-trained mind.

However that may be, the prevailing ideas of the two territories, and the preoccupations with which individuals were encumbered, differed, and hence those messages are couched in different idioms. Yet we must not be deceived by the difference in the packaging into supposing that the Masters' messages were generically different. They had similar objects in view. In both of them human beings' estimates of what was good for the species were accepted as a fundamental guide. Neither met the question, 'How do you know (without prophetic/mystical insight) that the conduct recommended will lead to the freedom alleged?' They proceeded as if the answer was self-evident. Self-control leads to autonomy and therefore to moral responsibility. Both presumed a readiness to make a commitment, to stop wavering, to make some investment. Neither was concerned with the world's estimates of what might be good behaviour: they offered formulas of conduct which every one of their hearers had the option to discard. Each individual exercises an 'existentialist' option; avoids self-deception; takes care of ultimate realities, and discovers his/her own needs.[1] The principal clue lies in what he/she loathes. That provides the answer (*see* Appendix III, p. 130).

1 Cf. Gerard Hughes, *Moral Decisions* (London: Darton, Longman & Todd, 1980).

23

AIMS AND HOPES

NEITHER the Buddha nor Jesus needed to experiment in ethical thinking, to find out whether his scheme worked. Neither, when satisfied he had found his answer, needed to preach, or to face the incredulity, and the jealousy of others. What were their hopes? Jesus saw himself as God's son, adopted and proclaimed as such (*Mt 3:17*), confirmed by miraculous powers, which some said must need the collaboration of a demon. As God's son he was his agent (*see* p. 58), and must do that work, taking in his stride the incomprehension and the barbed questions of others. The Buddha offered his formula to whosoever would take it upon being convinced. Both of them received extravagant expressions of satisfaction, for markets for their wares did exist. Both believed that if the resulting freedom were to be grasped humanity would be enlightened indefinitely.

The Buddha insisted that his hearers should reflect and confirm that their findings and his agreed. Everyone must work out his own salvation (cf. *P 2:12–13; 1C 9:24–7*). Following the Hebraic idiom Jesus took those of his hearers who were at all sympathetic as his 'flock', and regarded himself as responsible (*Mt 18:13; J 10:11*) for their spiritual welfare. The Buddha did what had to be done by argument, and over forty-five years expounded the framework of his monks' common living, and their relationships with the householders and their families. His relations with the state were also well worked out. He did not allow a conflict to occur between his *sangha* and the state; whereas Jesus did contemplate such a tragedy, putting the demands of God above those of the state. Suffering was therefore contemplated, despite the employment of tact. As his pupils opted for deprivation they opted for possible persecution from the state.

Both agreed in expecting that a convert would work smoothly with all righteous people, avoiding aggression, and taking without resentment whatever scorn might arise. He aimed to be prosperous for others without force or fraud; his hope was to be left alone sufficiently to achieve this.

Neither Jesus nor the Buddha contemplated the state's taking over the religious community, becoming responsible for it. This could happen if the fears and hopes of believers enticed them into trading with strangers whom they would not presume to judge (*1C 5:12–13*) and might even come to approve of (*R 12:17–18*). Such a bargain is onerous. The state will take its toll, not least by infusing an incongruous sense of power into the religious who have obtained its aid. They begin to find nothing absurd in comporting themselves as rulers. Paul's precept, to be subject to 'authorities' (*R 13:1, 5*), did not include the latter's ideologies. Self-righteousness and intolerance soon arise, and from them flow repression, inquisition, and the horrors of a pseudo-conformity based not on conscience but on complicity.

24

METHODS AND TECHNIQUES

A SYSTEM based on fear of rebirth, and a system based on a fear of hell, have something in common in that both formulas depend on illusions. There is neither rebirth (except in the metaphorical sense at *J 3:5*), nor hell. But these mitigate the self-centredness of personal decision-making. The methods share two other important features, which do not derive from illusion.

First, that which one hates and fears in life serves as a motivation to behave consistently without it (Appendix III, p. 130). For example, one who hates unreliability in others will be saved by treating others reliably. The illusions I referred to are echoes in mythical form of those common hatreds and fears. One who fears disappointment is saved by never disappointing others, and so on.

Next we have the discovery that whatever ill a person may have thought and done, the ensuing and 'deserved' retribution can be *cancelled*. A change of heart, shown by repentance, recompense, admission (confession) and the recognition that the fault has been admitted (confessed), will necessarily affect the future for a Buddhist. This is because there is no self to carry an accumulated sequence of moral deserts from day to day. The self is defined from moment to moment, and its moral stance at death helps to determine whether another birth ensues and if so with what prospects. The person whose *karma* is rendered infructuous (in plain English, his deserved destiny is counteracted) by this strange but delightful chemistry does *not* return to an evil life but continues in the realization, his stream-entering, or the later stages (*see* pp. 28, 31).

Similarly in primitive Christianity, indeed from the Baptist's time, repentance, already called for by the Old Testament (*Ps 14:1–3; Is 59:7–12*), was presumed to be accepted by God. It would not only put an end to diseases arising from unexpiated sins, but also will, if restitution is made, fit the former sinner for heaven. A new creature comes into existence (*2C 5:17; E 4:24*), another kind of rebirth. Wiped clean, as it were, the dog does not return to its vomit (*2Pe 2:21–2*), though if that *does* happen a strategy to reclaim him may be forthcoming (cf. *H 6:4–8; 2Pe 2:20*).

These very similar ideas contrast with Jewish notions. There we find a running balance of sins and good deeds kept in the heavenly books to determine a person's fate. More simply, a man has the fate of the righteous if the majority of his deeds are good. This fits a book-keeping mentality, and has much to be said for it. The Buddhist and Christian solutions are more generous, and tend to encourage repentance, provided this is coupled with re-education. The later Christian idea of confession followed by absolution, which requires, in usual circumstances, a priest–confessor to give the absolution, confirms at any rate that retribution for misdeeds may be remitted or cancelled.

But what if the individual, as often today, does not believe in sin, and sees no need to repent, except of a project which has gone wrong? It is known for a person, whose behaviour has been challenged, to insist that he cannot be blamed, or that whatever blame there is can be ignored, or that no reparation would change the situation. There speaks a member of an individualistic society. Such a latitude is not at home in collective societies, where one is brought up to accept the reactions of elders without question.

To such contumacy the Buddha has an answer: 'Does your method obtain the approval of those whose opinions you esteem? Does it lead you to a result which is to your ultimate advantage?' If the answer is in the affirmative the conduct is at least allowable, though it may be free of merit. Paul likewise is concerned that in dilemmas each must be assured in his own mind (*R 14:5*). The Buddha never thought of compulsion in matters of conscience; and the Christian history of tyranny, leading to horrors and even deaths, is taking a long time to live down.

Of our two Masters one believed a course of action was demanded by reality (what *X* feared provided the clue to *X*'s escape). It was neglected by unenlightened people at their peril. The other thought the Word of God was to be followed out, relying on observation and a prophetic reading of holy texts. Paul's elaboration of this at *R 2:17–24*[1] shows that there is a wide gap between literal observance of the Law and what an active conscience would demand. But both systems achieved, for the time being, much the same result, subject to the handicaps built into their environments, all traceable, perhaps, back to a common human nature.

---

1 Derrett at *NTS* 40/4 (1994), 558–71.

25

WORSHIP AND PRACTICE

THE individual remains the true focus of decision-making, even though the Buddha saw himself as a teacher, and Jesus as shepherd. The sheep will stray. It mocks both parties to draw the teacher several sizes larger than the pupil/ suppliant.[1] The joy of release from perplexity, whether in Israel, in the Greek world, in India or beyond, found expression in dramatic behaviour, *sc.* excessive generosity to the *sangha* in the East, or pouring ointment on Jesus (*Mk 14:3*), or entering into previously unheard of sexual unions (*1C 5:1*), or 'prophecies' or 'tongues' in the primitive Church. Claims to ignore the distinctions between people leads in the case of Christians to phenomena which could please Church leaders (e.g. the kiss of peace), while some called for repression. Worship, passing beyond the observances of the synagogue, led to institutions, to church-structures, to the worshippers facing towards a common object, or, in the case of Buddhists, circumambulation of a cult object, instead of being occupied with each other, and with the world outside. Those who made the largest contribution carried the most weight in the community, so bypassing equality. Is worship an arena to develop self-command, or a medium of entertainment? If both, the presence of the second may prejudice the first.

Gradually the believers felt the need to express their own contributions, at the expense of their dependency on the Saviour (*J 4:42*). They (and I think of females especially) wanted to do something for the Master, what they could (*Mk 14:8a*). Veneration of the Buddhist holy places led in time to cults whose relation to Buddhist ethics was minimal. One could show one's joy in what amounted to a tourist trip, hanging up garlands and watering trees, or picnicking. Turning Jesus into God's only-begotten Son in the sense of a divine being (*1Ti 3:16*) was a mistake, perhaps inevitable in the hellenistic world. The effects could have been conjectured. Where the possibility of such an error existed the risk should not have been taken. The Buddha's quite rational self-praise asked for this anomaly, and Jesus' scarcely concealed self-elevation to the role of God's counsellor (*L 10:22; J 1:3, 14*) partly excuses a worship which becomes an embarrassment. To have discovered a great thing is not the same as to have invented it.

Worship of Buddhas and Bodhisattvas, again, has lessened awareness of the need to acquire merit by adhering to the Eightfold Path. Indeed the grace of a Bodhisattva is required because the attainment of *arahan* status has seemed irrel-

1 *The Sermon on the Mount. Drawings by H.J. Knowles* (London: Ivor Nicholson, 1935).

evant. The prospect of becoming a Bodhisattva by devotion to the Buddha has attracted many a Buddhist who had little respect for the *sangha*, and *stūpas* became more interesting than monasteries. To have been an actual hearer of Gotama became an undistinguished status. The texts we have been consulting became mere cult objects, while legends became more interesting.

Worship of Christ as one of the Holy Trinity, and the shifting of faith from one focus to another, have distracted attention from the Ten Commandments and the Sermon on the Mount. That worship elevated priests and construed the ceremony of the Bread and Wine (cf. *L 22:17–20*) as a priestly activity. Various forms of sanctification have taken the place of obedience to precepts. Means of grace have been invented which make conformity to Jesus' teaching less relevant. Justification by faith (sc. in theologians, since they decide in what one should have faith), has led to a severance between practice and belief; while the practice of priestly absolution takes attention off the peril of sinning at the time of the sin.

Paul's insistence on faith rather than observances such as are laid down in the Law (*R 1:17; G 3:11*) was originally an attempt to point out that conscience determines one's chances of salvation, not external obedience to ritual or even charitable work (like leaving unharvested corn in the field for the poor to take). In this sense he can say that what does not proceed from faith is sin (*R 14:23*). Paul cannot have imagined that his doctrine would be used to discard interest in what people actually did (*see* above p. 60), an absurdity which one level of the mind (*see* p. 115) will readily embrace; nor that certain churches would decide that *governments* would never be subject to Christ's precepts.

Gotama did not believe in gods except as an embellishment and source of metaphor. That he should be worshipped would never have crossed his mind. Jesus certainly never required to be worshipped as a divine being. As bearer of the truth, he had a divine commission, and he should be listened to as one who mediated God's instructions. Faith that he had released Israel from her (former) sins is a doctrine having no bearing upon this whatsoever. It can be queried whether the practice of the two ethical systems in their primitive forms did not lose cogency and efficiency because of these unfortunate developments.

The ancient Romans, whom the Jews classed as 'idolaters', certainly offered 'worship' to statues of gods, heroes, emperors, their own ancestors, and 'great men', whose birthdays they celebrated (Seneca, *Moral Letters*, 64:9). The action expressed a genuine respect. But such behaviour was not a *substitute* for attention to what they stood for. The argument of 'iconoclasts' is trite: anxiety like mine arises when devotion to an icon, material or imaginary, absorbs energy which should be devoted to self-discipline.

26

ESCHATOLOGY AND MOTIVES

A SERIOUS error was made when it was believed that Gotama meant literally
what he said about heaven and hell. Rebirth may take place so promptly
that Gotama could say his friend had reached a point from which there was no
more returning to this earth. But the further-life or -lives are, as are Jesus' talk of
after-life banquets and hell (*Mt 22:10–13*), mere images to induce the hearer to
remodel his life. The psalmist says, 'Today if you will hear…' (*Ps 97:7; H 3:7*), i.e.
decision has to be made now, however long the ultimate Judgement may be de-
ferred. To motivate people to be wakeful and sober (*1T 5:6*), it is not sufficient to
promise this-worldly profit, since one profit can be weighed against another, and
different people rate profits differently. Hence eschatology (the study of the End
Time) is a device to attract, and to retain attention. Since Jesus' message could
not be improved upon (just as no *buddha* could improve upon the Buddha), it
follows that, for practical purposes, his time *is* the End Time. There will be no
better chances – or so his hearers supposed. Jesus himself took it that the power
of Satan was virtually ended already (*J 12:31, 16:11*).

To claim that Jesus was a deluded enthusiast who expected the End of the Age
after his death, in the lifetime of some of his hearers (*Mt 16:28*), and that Paul
was similarly deluded, so as to distort his teaching (*1C 7:29;* cf. *Ac 2:17; H 1:2;
1Pe 4:7*), suggests that in Jesus' lifetime, and for a while after, his believers expected the Son of Man would come, as Daniel predicted (*Dn 7:13*), and the Age
would be wrapped up, during 'this' generation (*Ac 24:33–6*). When some died
before this Coming it was wondered whether they had missed something of value
(*1T 4:14–15*). Their disappointment was alarming.

But this is to assume that believers were naive. The motive to behave according
to Jesus' precepts cannot be found from seeking worldly advantages, for if one
fled worldly disadvantages one fled the advantages, hence a change of lifestyle.
Motivation derives from a timeless perspective. Paul himself exhorted his readers
to behave 'decently' now as if the day of reckoning were actually here, using the
simile of daytime sobriety as contrasted with the night-time drunkenness which
is ordinary life (*R 13:12–13; 1T 5:5–7*). If one is still at home in the 'flesh' one is
exiled from the Lord; nevertheless one must be acceptable to him in point of
conduct (not a nude faith) even while one is in this 'exile' (*2C 5:6, 9–10*). The
individual's quality stands to be assessed *whenever* accounts are taken, as is still
the traditional Jewish expectation. *When* is not important (*L 17:20*). One must

live as if it will be tomorrow – hence we have Jesus' alarming parables of the returning householder, which are a better guide to his eschatology than much mythological detail found elsewhere. The theme is richly illustrated.[1] 'You do not know the time...' (*Mt 25:13;* cf. *24:43–4*). And by the same token no one can say it is at any indefinite remove! It is an *as-if* concept, as I have explained. And this is made obvious by the allusion to the time of Noah, when people were enjoying themselves, 'until the flood came and took them all away' (*Mt 24:37–9*). Accounts may be inspected best when unexpectedly. 'One of the illusions is that the present hour is not the critical, decisive hour...No man has learned anything rightly, until he know that every day is Doomsday...Do not refuse the employment which the hour brings you, for one more ambitious.'[2]

---

1 *Mt 24:50; Mk 13:36; L 12:36–7;* cf. *Mk 14:40.* Paul says that *now* is the vital time (*R 8:21–5*).
2 R.W. Emerson, *Society and Solitude* (1870), §7.

27

ACHIEVEMENTS

I N spite of illusions, numbers of people have tried to live according not merely to cosmopolitan ideas of goodness, e.g. not to kill, to steal, or to commit adultery, but according to religious principles – not resting content with compliance with prohibitions. Even those who have not tried are sometimes tweaked by conscience (*R 2:15*), finding excuses for pursuing their urges into action. The theory that people can control themselves for an 'unseen' reason, define it how you will, and that they should do so, e.g. for their own 'self-respect', or their 'good name' (*Ecclesiastes 7:1*), is borne out by experience.

They will be interested in those innovators who put fear and boredom to good use, turned conventions upside down, and, like true discoverers, merited respect. Other discoveries may lie ahead. They too may be greeted with ridicule and suspicion. One recollects the progress of medicine; much now taken for granted was, when introduced, dismissed as quackery. And the practitioner who did not bleed a patient for any disorder, or failed to trepan a patient with a headache, was thought to be wanting in attention to his duty.

Not the least interesting feature of the Buddhist and Christian teachings is their lame character. How much ground they do not cover! Nothing is said about *diet*, if one excludes Jesus' ridicule of food as a source of impurity as compared with moral filth (*Mt 15:11*), and neglects Paul's interestingly subjective view of uncleanness (*R 14:14*). Neither the Buddha nor Jesus discuss 'white lies'. These (uttered to lovers, patients, robbers, etc.) are noticed in the *Laws of Manu* (*8:104, 112*), and therefore figured in ancient Indian casuistry. They have no role in Buddhist casuistry (*BD 2:166–70*). The explanation may be that in neither Master's eyes are 'white' lies serious attempts to deceive, and as such no rigorous attitude towards them was demanded of a public prone to duplicity. If a deontological system would be capable of requiring absolute truthfulness, let the heavens fall, it is interesting that neither Master demanded that. And a similar explanation may avail other gaps in their teaching.

The arts and history are ignored as studies; Jesus is sarcastic about an elaborate piece of architecture. The duties of rulers barely figure, and were obviously hardly worth considering. The administration of justice is only alluded to as a source of woe, probably because no known system of courts was respectable (cf. *L 18:2, 6*). Rights in general are overlooked – perhaps because their societies were duty-orientated. And, where the handicapped and the destitute are mentioned, no interest in their long-term good is shown. Both the Masters were interested in generosity (in Jesus' case alms) as behaviour of value to the donor.

Thus we may be thankful that we are not called upon to discuss Jesus' economics, or the Buddha's politics outside his commonplace recommendations. Both teachers were pacifists to the same extent and for the same reason: killing is an injury to the supersensory interests of the killer, and all violence can be judged in the same light. Waste of the riches of the environment is a vice in Buddhist eyes; but Jesus' position is a little obscure, and a guess is allowable.

The earth and the riches thereof are the Lord's (*1C 10:26; Ps 24:1*), and God is the owner of wild life (*Ps 50:10–11*). All things belong to Christians (cf. *Ps 8:6–7*), but *they* belong to Christ (*1C 3:22–3*). Even if the environment was not a problem in Jesus' day, the idea of stewardship, which appears in his teaching, can be thought to be relevant. In all things Christians must 'bear fruit' for God (*J 15:5, 8, 16*).

An important parable, preserved in two forms (*Mt 25:14–30; L 19:11–27*), deals with man's duty to account for his stewardship. This idea of accountability occurs in several places in the New Testament. In the parable an employer who was also a capitalist entrusted slices of capital to employees (who contributed nothing but their skill) in order to be invested on his behalf. He was eventually angry with one who refused to invest. The latter returned the capital, unimproved, on the ground that the capitalist was a skinflint, and so it was not worth his own while to service an investment. He was deprived of the money, on the maxim, 'To him who has shall be given, and from him who has not shall be taken away what [little] he has.' The parable is not about money and the market. It is not a comment on the talent for business.[1] It is about employing one's legitimate opportunities. It is about work and getting on with it. On that basis every facility is to be used by human beings so as to make themselves profitable for the Creator. One can argue that whatever imperils the regeneration of nature is repugnant to Jesus' understanding of what opportunities are for. This implies a long view of every undertaking. The short view is likely to be characteristic of the 'wicked'. The long view consists with the perception that human beings exist for the whole and not the whole for them (Plato, *Laws* 903CD), and though the two Masters' teachings are subjective in aim, they heartily concurred with that perception.

---

1 Cyrus, emperor of Persia, ridiculed the Greeks for providing a place in each city where men might cheat one another on oath (Herodotus, *hist* 1:153). This was not social satire but snobbery (Persian nobles did not traffic or chaffer).

PART FOUR

CONCLUSION

28

MUST MATTERS REST THERE?

OUR two Masters belong to periods as remote as the fourth century BC and the first century AD respectively, and no compelling analysis of behaviour has emerged since, which could be claimed to be furnished with a new set of precepts remotely comparable in appeal with theirs. Philosophical theories dressed up as objective enquiries agreeing substantially with the Christian ethic have emerged, but their authors never eclipsed those Masters, whose moral teachings have survived when every miraculous element of their biographies has been dismissed.

If the systems had inherent flaws, e.g. not preventing their sinking back into the parent religion from which they emerged; the tendency to admire the teacher and to ignore his teaching; the tendency to water down his teaching to make it conform to the 'world'; and the tendency to bypass his teaching by providing substitutes allegedly in the spirit of the original – if all those flaws could have been foreseen and forestalled, does that diminish the wisdom of the founders? It seems not. That Jesus and his followers warned of false teachers and even false Messiahs[1] was not enough. The Masters' lives and not a little of their teachings interest the satirist. Yet the prestige of the systems has never faltered. Attempts to expound both flow from the presses; while human behaviour remains virtually untouched.

The idea, meanwhile, that Buddhism is impracticable has been rejected firmly by Tachibana, who was in a position to know. The idea that the Sermon on the Mount is impracticable has been ridiculed by me. It is reminiscent of the practice of the *hasīdīm*, who lived prosperously despite their refusal to soil themselves or their assets with immorality or illegality.[2] Both systems are practicable, though not without cost. Matters can hardly rest with the compromises of the late twentieth century. Courage may emerge and not merely amongst such as were once enthusiastic for Buddhist renunciation or Christian messianism.

Will innovators arise who can so neatly turn to the individual's advantage his fears and his incompetence, which was the Buddha's and Jesus' secret? This is a formula upon which the centuries have not been able to improve. One does not

---

1 *Mt 7:15, 24:24; 2C 11:13; 2Ti 4:3; 2Pe 2:1; 1J 4:1.*

2 Derrett, *Sermon on the Mount* (Northampton: Pilkington, 1994), 88–93. If a *hasīd* borrowed from one of two deceased persons and no one could remember which, he would pay the heirs of both. They would not refuse, since they could not prove that their antecedent had not lent to him.

have to opt to become a god in order to try. Lambert Schmithausen has devised an adaptation of the Buddhist precept against killing living things, including plants, to meet modern requirements. Christians are studying how to 'marry' homosexuals,[1] and ingenuity is not exhausted.

1 A.E. Harvey, *Promise or Pretence? A Christian's Guide to Sexual Morals* (London: SCM Press, 1994). 110–15.

29

'GREAT IS TRUTH AND IT SHALL PREVAIL'

M Y quotation (cf. *1 Esdras 4:35*) is used to bolster propaganda, but few will quarrel with me when I suggest that lies, fantasies, make-believe and false psychology cannot survive for ever. To support a mythological religion with spurious appeals to reason bores us. As science progresses, and not least on its psychological front, religion can be fringed with mythology only as an embellishment. The wall-paper cannot keep the wall from falling. The metaphor of the badly plastered wall was used in the Old Testament; Paul used the passage unpleasantly (*Ac 23:3*). The wall has been a long time falling, but fall it must.

On the other hand if the Buddha happened upon truth, and Jesus preached truth, namely that motivation for good is concealed in human beings' complaints against life as they know it, their teachings must prevail, whether or not under the name of their teachings.

Our principal object in comparing the Buddha's and Jesus' experiences is not to make invidious use of their differences, but to reveal what a stroke it was on both their parts to expose the motivation latent in mankind. They paint with a broad brush. Praise and blame is lavished by Jesus, much in the style used by his forefathers and contemporaries: black or white, bad or good. 'Contrivances', intentions, are worthy or unworthy, meritorious or unmeritorious, not taking the short and casuistical, but the long view. His hearers will not have quarrelled with that. The Buddha, who had little time for general blame (except of his foolish rivals) or praise, is bolder. He expected standards of behaviour to be asserted and disseminated, as well amongst the sophisticates of princely courts as amongst forest tribes who had never forgiven the incursions of the Aryans a millennium before. To accept the Four Noble Truths with their attendant Noble Eightfold Path would free one from the wheel of birth, death, and rebirth. Jesus' reversal of human expectations would free the believer from not only hell, or the wrath of God, but from all fear of them. Both Masters sought to correct their contemporaries' and future generations' perception of the value of life as they lived it. Human motivation implies a capacity to compare and to choose, and this fact our Masters exploited. 'Choose life' was already a commandment (*Dt 30:19*).

Did they estimate correctly? If not, their systems have only a curiosity value, like much religious debris with which history is cluttered. If yes, the survival of both systems through centuries of corruption during which they have been travestied is no accident, the arrow has reached its target (p. 88 n.2). The harvest (p. 72) is a reality and the wheat must still be beaten out of the chaff.

30

TWO PLANES OF EXISTENCE

IT is obvious that the Masters understood human beings to exist in two senses, as it were on two planes. There were their ideal selves, which should meet their own and other people's requirements; and there were their actual selves, puzzling from time to time to themselves and to others.

The first self was imaginary. If there were angels they would be like that. The second, which is all too real, may be called, disparagingly, 'fleshly' or 'worldly'. A dualistic system of thought (the powers of Light fight the powers of Darkness) will find human beings open to the wiles of Satan, who will never be ignored in a dualistic discourse on behaviour (*see* pp. 64, 87). The imaginary self would correspond in kind to that required by parents or guardians. It is only a step from that to imagine that God (*E 2:10*) has similar requirements (*R 8:8*), and that, in falling short of an ideal, one disappoints him. In an a-theistic system one falls short of one's own transcendental goal. This (unverifiable) position is now regarded in some quarters as neurotic, but it is intelligible.

A connection can be made between this dichotomy of selves and the problems arising during and after puberty. Paul, in whose remarks a hysterical timbre can be detected, never recovered from the discovery that what he wanted to do he did not do, and vice versa (*R 7*). We guess that this had to do with the area of mating, with its penumbra of observations, desires and contrivances, from which, for example, a eunuch might be exempted.

One speaks, emotionally, of being enslaved by desires (R *6:16–20; Tit 3:3*), so that a fornicator, one may claim, sins against his own body (*1C 6:18*). Paul was aware, as a Jew, that liability to perform the Law of Moses arose for the first time at puberty. The pre-pubertal stage was both Law-free (*R 7:9*) and, if one interpreted the Law idealistically and perfectionistically, sin-free. Cultures which do not impose a liability to perform religious commandments for the first time when puberty occurs (as if on the stroke of a gong) will find it difficult to understand how the pre-pubertal child can be sin-free, and that to be suddenly fixed with knowledge of the Law amounts to a death sentence (*R 7:5, 7*), there being a curse upon anyone who does not perform *all* the requirements of the Law (*G 3:10; Dt 27:26*). Nor can they fathom how life in the world can be represented as death through sins (*E 2:1–2, 5*). However, it is from this standpoint one may understand Paul's strange assertion, that the Law engenders a sinful condition, making one aware, e.g., of what is covetousness, so that for the first time (*R 7:7–8*) one knows that one is coveting!

From our point of view what matters is that from unaccountable desires, sometimes externally generated, arising dramatically after puberty, one can generalize. One can claim that a whole range of tendencies towards sin refuses to be subject either to reason or to commandment. Self-consciousness is really not enough (cf. *R 2:27–9, 7:6–13*). If sexual activity, and all that is associated with it, illustrates the realm of the fleshly self, and prevents the realization of the 'angelic' self, then a dualistic culture will find many sinful tendencies beyond the reach of religious teaching – unless, that is to say, the individual is so powerfully affected by faith in a saviour that the earthly self is converted. What the Law was not designed to reach, for all its allusions to the escape from Egypt, the faith just mentioned might reach. Many will confirm that strong and apt emotional stimuli will affect behaviour which was previously quietly controlled by unconscious forces, inaccessible to admonition or example. Once set free from a burden (*R 8:2*), from the 'reign' of sin (*R 6:12, 14*), one can become addicted to 'righteousness' (*R 6:17–18*).

The person who reacted to such a stimulus would find himself living in much the same material circumstances, yet unlimited by them. God's offers can now make sense, and his rewards become available in an imaginary sense irrespective of verification. It is possible to speak as if 'our commonwealth is in heaven' (*P 3:10*). The prisoner has a plane on which he feels a free man, and vicissitudes of circumstances lose their significance (*4:12–13*). It is possible to claim that such a programme is a licence to oppressors (e.g. slave-owners) to misuse those subject to their power; but the programme is not political, nor in the usual sense of the word social: it is directed to the building up of subjective fitness to face what life has to offer. Paul, unable to cope with his dilemmas, believed only supernatural aid could ultimately release him (*R 7:24*).

Speaking the language of men (cf. *R 3:5, 6:19*), I notice that people function in a businesslike, responsible way, willing to account for their actions (or lack of action) with explanations which their fellows will be likely to accept. They can say, 'You too...'; and yet in their thoughts they have experiences which their training(s), and their reasons, reject. To take one illustration: all of a sudden an outbreak of 'child abuse' occurs. It can be argued that miscreants have crossed the barrier between fantasy and responsible social life. An appetite which they were aware of became, when for once they were not accountable for their behaviour, an actuality. The crime of rape is an even better example. Challenged with their crimes the offenders say they meant no harm: quite so, they meant to gratify themselves, to gratify a non-rational self.

Paradoxes emerge. It is noteworthy that later portions of New Testament literature refer to 'lusts' frequently: conversion had by no means repressed or exorcized them. Anathemas against those who purchased too cheaply the respectability which Christianity offered were useless. Such paradoxes may well evoke a conjecture.

Just as different areas of the brain control different areas of the body, and different activities (e.g. singing as opposed to speaking), so any one person can have simultaneously contradictory instincts and desires, reactions and responses. This would make him impotent, unless a considerable area of activity (e.g. digestion), probably the oldest in evolutionary terms, was unconscious. The involuntary nervous system is at least as important as the voluntary. The point of having an 'unconscious' is that it remains unconscious, leaving traces of which the subject, and others, become aware in retrospect. The unconscious has its own history, though it is doubtful whether it ages. Experiences in babyhood, in adolescence, and even later build up to colour the powerhouse of the personality, the conscious mind being left with the task of directing operations, both interpreting and justifying actions of which it is not the true author. It is along such lines that Buddhists rejoice to see their Blessed One denying that there is such a thing as the self.

One can understand another person with the heart better than with the brain. A lover may forgive the beloved anything – until the love vanishes. This quasi-maternal love is the calculation of the unconscious, not the conscious mind. To the unconscious the no-hoper may be the ideal comrade. Friends predict the union spells disaster; and when it does, the unconscious discovers, without the aid of reason, that comradeship has vanished. There was an entity (we call it the self) which was to be supported, and the unconscious is selfish. When support is no longer needed (on those terms) from X, X (a worthy person) is dropped. Reason exclaims, but the unconscious knows better.

This is only an exploration of our problem. The point is clear: when the preacher talks to X he is talking to a complex being, the senses admitting information, another organ evaluating it, yet another determining whether to act upon it, and yet another far more powerful than these, which decides whether or not it 'fits'. Hypocrisy is found everywhere, since people may do good works out of unworthy motives (P $1:15$, 17), and one fails to notice one's hypocrisy since different parts of the brain are involved.

One knows of church-goers who abandon their church because of an untimely word from the minister, the death of a relative or friend, an emotional attachment to a believer of another faith, or, less frequently, an unfriendly exposure of the church's creed. The unconscious determines what company 'fits', and in what contexts: the rational explanations are often a smoke-screen, deceiving the subject as well as others.

Hence if Jesus' or the Buddha's schemes of training appeal to people it is because they achieve effects corroborated by the unconscious, to be verified later by the conscious mind. Their continual popularity in spite of institutional incompetence, the diversion of energy into irrelevant undertakings, and the systematic neglect of the training itself, must be explicable in terms of their appeal to the unconscious.

The unconscious can never give an account of itself. Its functions in evolution are hypothetical. Advertisers *know* that it has tastes, and can exploit these. In our area its demands have never been calibrated. But from results we can infer something.

Its tastes include the religious, since it can approve behaviour which is contrary to the principles by which secular life is conducted. It may be a function of the unconscious to apprehend the 'unseen', the factor to which we have been referring, the unlimited plane of existence which takes ideas of immortality seriously, for it knows that the flesh must die (*R 8:6, 13*).

The collective and its perpetuation, the tribe, collaboration, co-achievement, are factors which became crucial when human beings emerged amongst 'primates'. To enhance these is to put the individual into harmony with his remote ancestors, but not his *most* remote, who did not develop the ability to collaborate in joint ventures except as a long process of learning. Yet the step was taken, and irrevocably. It is possible the unconscious remembers. Even abhorrent rivals are now cousins, even brothers (*R 14:10*). The evocation of 'brother', that strange blend of collaboration and rivalry, supports my hypothesis. To point out that a neighbour is or ought to be a kind of brother, irrespective of his merits, is to talk to the unconscious rather than the conscious mind which merely processes the sounds. The latter may have objections, the former none. Both the Buddha and Jesus in effect tackled the question, how humankind may become whole, all parts of the brain working together to a propitious end. The non-confrontational person will be a happier person. Will his mediocre finances diminish his happiness?

31

INTEGRITY

THAT human beings are not automatically integrated units was observed by Paul, but the fact need not be deplored as it was by him. We must commence with things as they are. In the area we have been discussing human nature has hardly changed from his day to ours. The ideal Christian character is universally admired, though seldom met with. The prestige of the Jesus-system is testified to by the curious fact that, while born Christians have been poor advertisements for Jesus, whole areas of the world have felt the need to re-present themselves as 'every bit as good as, if not better than, Christians'. The damage done by this make-believe seems to have been minimal.

Internal revolutions in expression, taste, and not seldom substance took place in India, which throughout the nineteenth century became so used to presenting itself as 'at least as good as Christianity without the intolerance', that the true character of Hinduism as it stood at the beginning of the century was forgotten even by Hindus themselves. Stranger still, Judaism has presented itself in an in-gratiating light. Not under any obligation to be 'Christian', Jews have tried to show not only that Christianity started as an offshoot from Judaism (which is true), but that every virtue it has ever possessed was and is present in the Judaisms of today. Where modern Israeli behaviour affronts Christians Israel feels obliged to defend herself.

Even stranger, Muslims, whose militant faith reflected the insufficiencies, for certain Arab groups, of Judaism and Christianity, go out of their way to claim that Islam has every virtue which Christians could conceivably manifest, with more besides. Buddhism alone successfully evades this tendency. It has found Christianity superfluous in territory after territory.

This noticeable general testimony, coupled with the fact that the Masters are revered even by those who cannot follow them, should confirm that the message, which deliberately overturned ordinary presuppositions, has something to teach, though embarrassing to isolate and demonstrate. I submit its appeal lies in its offer to homologize, to integrate the individual's mind, bringing the unconscious and the conscious into that sort of harmony which, say Golden Age fantasists, our forefathers once enjoyed. The Buddhist fable of the steady decline from pri-meval abundance into the present Age, where each must fight for himself, sup-ports me in the view that even the Buddha's disciples were aware that they were re-creating on a small scale what was once the common heritage of all.

How would this function? Humility, non-aggression, working to employ one's skills in unobjectionable ways, living on a minimum, showing friendliness and compassion, avoiding conflict rather than penalizing, all this may well turn out to be consistent with a 'low standard of living', and ultra-piety and modest circumstances tend to go together. It may indeed prove difficult for believers to produce telephone directories in alphabetical order on time. But the tone of society could improve. It may be argued that scientific advances will not be made which require the investment of capital normally obtained by exploiting the public's needs, or the bounty of nature. But this has to be proved, and great discoveries have been made on a single culture-dish.

The assumption that the maximum number of individuals must be kept alive indefinitely with the maximum of technology is characteristic of this age. Neither to the Buddha nor to Jesus was the length of an individual's life of the slightest consequence. And when the expectation of life was low, as it has remained from their days until quite recently, a concentration on *living well* made a special appeal.[1]

---

1 Cf. Plato *Gorgias* 512 DE

32

THE IMPORTANCE OF THE INDIVIDUAL

NEITHER Jesus nor the Buddha taught anything about Rights. Even Human Rights were below their horizon. They were not concerned with man's duty to man, still less man's duty to woman in any modern sense. 'Husbands love your wives [irrespective of their merits]' (*E 5:25; Co 3:19*), though backed by a religious symbol, is a somewhat pathetic exhortation – one wonders why it was necessary, and whom it impressed? The Masters' precepts were directed to the individual subject, who had total freedom to neglect them. The idea of compelling adherence to a formula was foreign to them. The phrase, 'Compel them to come in' (*L 14:23*), meant simply that otherwise neglected people are to have their modesty, and their pessimism, overcome, so that they too share in what the Creator has in store for them. A fantasy? Yes, but language the unconscious understands: 'There is a plane, on which all you *really* want can be supplied to you. Believe this and nothing of value will be withheld from you.' Reason does not support this; the faith of the unconscious does, for it remembers childhood's confidence. Therefore crime is not the answer to shortage, nor is scrounging.

The Masters directed their efforts towards the individual. Living in a collective society as he did, his fears and strangulated hopes supply motivation. To recognize the importance of the individual (cf. *Mt 10:31*) marks a step in the development of freedom and responsibility.[1] He is good to other people not for their sakes but for his own. They benefit from his renunciation of greed or craving. Inter-group behaviour would seem impervious to this technique. But groups are made up of individuals, and their group-behaviour (which reveals features of the unconscious) will respond to teachings which speak to the unconscious. Inter-group behaviour does not figure in the Masters' teaching, apart from the Buddha's prudential admonitions, which do not concern us, and Jesus' contemptuous references to wars (*Mt 24:6*).

> It was not the community with which [Jesus] was primarily concerned...[O]ne of his chief advances on earlier morality was that he broke away from the concept of the group as the governing factor in human action. Men had value in the sight of God not as units in a society but as individual beings. This is the constitutive principle in the social ethic of Jesus, and it is this which in all times has made it a revolutionary power.[2]

1 Gustafson, *op. cit.*, 102-3.

2 Ernest F. Scott at E. Hershey Sneath, ed., *The Evolution of Ethics* (New Haven: Yale University Press, 1927), 284. Would one be right to detect here a perception specially open to Americans?

One is good to other people for one's own sake, and for one's own sake one abstains from injuring them. For one's own sake one takes care not to connive at another's faults. This covers inter- as well as intra-group behaviour.

One who obeys the Commandments (*Mk 10:21*) may well go further and give all he has to propagate the truth – or, as in a famous instance, he may not. But who knows how the dilemma will be resolved in his case or in others'? Unless an individual adopts the teaching, presented to him in an idiom he can comprehend, society cannot obtain the benefits which the Masters conferred. One asks, why then did they have to confer it?

How did egoism, rivalry, snobbism, self-righteousness, exploitation occur? The instincts to preserve the self, to hoard, to repel aggressors, and to forestall attacks, existed before the era of collaboration in hunting. Collaboration grew to channel aggression, to aid food-gathering of a new type. The movement away from an amorphous group to artificial groups, the 'nuclear family' or even smaller units, is a further stage. When the dangers of extolling the potential of the exploiter became visible, with apocalyptic results attached to unchecked progress along that path, our Masters produced their solutions.

So long as people at large will admire wealth-accumulators irrespective of their chosen methods, there is an incentive to continue in fratricidal strife. But there could be greater success in not accumulating, not exploiting others, whereby one escapes from competition without loss of subsistence, and both internal and external conflicts are minimized. The ancient world knew contented slaves (an illustration we should hardly have chosen); and unambitious social groupings, too, might be obviously contented.

The virtue of the systems offered by the Buddha and by Jesus is that they tender a challenge demanding on every enterprising mind, and worthy of every high achiever. Success in it widens the scope of admiration which he or she can earn, and which neither Jesus nor the Buddha questioned. Instead of the signals and symbols of ascribed status they can, in undistinguished garb, be congratulated by those who are not easily deceived by appearances, by which (appearances) indeed we too should not judge (*J 7:24*).

APPENDIX I

OBSERVANCES, WITH SPECIAL
REFERENCE TO BAPTISM

R ELIGIOUS observances are relatively easy (one does not offer more than one can perform) and they make no demands on the conscience. Hostility to them is found in Jesus' teaching (*see* above, p. 67), and the Buddha's, where it is an article of faith: no one may count himself a follower of the Buddha unless he renounces belief in the value of observances (p. 28). *The Laws of Manu*, too (*6:66–7*), is sceptical of observances. Yet the Buddha's objection to, for example, sacrifices (cf. *S 4:218–20*) was one of the complaints Brahmins had against him. In his view no moral conditions could be 'cleansed' by observances (*Sn 249*).

The Buddha's objections have not held over the centuries. Monks officiate at ceremonies containing rituals of various origins which are observances. It can be argued that the Pātimokkha ceremony,[1] performed twice a lunar month (full moon and new moon), is an observance. However, it is expected to be a searching of the conscience and could originally be interrupted unpredictably if one of the *sangha* remembered he had not confessed a fault on that long list. If his fault had not already been processed the *sangha* must notice it at once, for the purpose of the ceremony was to declare the *sangha* pure. This is not an observance carried out mechanically and bringing merit to the doer merely by the doing of it. The Buddha could use the term 'purification' metaphorically, but for him one could be 'purified' only by practising the *dhamma*. It is of interest that, despite Jewish obsession with rinsing and immersion, a *mental* cleansing by pious intention, irrespective of ritual observances, was once accepted by Yahweh as adequate at the prayer of Hezekiah in *2 Chronicles 30:17–20* – a text usually taken to endorse purifications.

Jesus did not object to the ceremony of baptism (cf. *Is 4:2–4*) utilized by John the Baptist in response to individuals' confession of sins and symbolizing repentance (*Mk 1: 4–5; cf. Ps 51*). It seems that at least on some occasions he practised it himself (*Mt 3:13–14*), even baptizing some who wished to confess their sins and commence a new life (*J 3:22, 26; cf. Ac 2:38*). Baptism does mime new creation. The ceremony is probably derived from total immersion usual in observant Jewish ritual life,[2] and thence especially in the ceremonies whereby a proselyte

---

1 Wang Pachow, *A Comparative Study of the Prātimoksa* (Santiniketan, 1955).

2 *Mk* 7:4; Josephus, *Life* 11,12; Mishnah, *Miq.* 6:3, 10:8; *A.Z.* 52b. Maimonides, *Book of the Commandments*, Positive Commandment 108. W. Brandt, *Die jüdischen Baptismen* (Giessen, 1910); B.J. Bamberger, *Proselytism in the Talmudic Period* (Hoboken NJ: Ktav, 1968); G. Alon, *Jews, Judaism, and the Classical World* (Jerusalem, 1977), 190–234. Stembaugh-Balch (1986), 60.

was inducted into Jewry.[1]

Immersion as a sign of entry into a new life, as it were from a womb, is intelligible. In Hinduism it is a rite of passage from studentship into the householder's stage of life,[2] or into renunciation of the world.[3] Nevertheless it was no more than a symbol,[4] publicly expressing a conscious intention. No one believed that washing would remove sin and crime, or protect against subsequent wrongdoing;[5] though the prehistoric metaphor of cleansing from sin was well known as such (*Pr 30:12; Is 1:16; Ez 36:25; Jas 4:8*). One knew that purification of the soul was achieved by creating proper judgements within it (Epictetus IV 11:5–8), a point of view the Buddha would have relished. If washing in water was thought to remove sin that would indeed be an objectionable observance.

Immersion arose in Brahminical ceremonies (cf. *Manu 2:176, 4:82*). The Buddha will have objected to immersion in the Ganges as a purificatory rite. It is a typical observance, with muttering of *mantras*. In spite of Rigveda I.23:22 people are not purified by immersion. From Brahminical rituals the idea spread of immersion in a river, or even in a well (*Manu 4:201, 203*), as a penance.[6] In the Buddha's day there were individuals and groups who practised daily, and even thrice-daily immersions, as a sign of asceticism; and there were those who stayed in water up to their necks for long periods.[7]

The Buddha asked comically whether such a practice was conducive to blissful attainment in conduct, in heart, and in intellect, not to speak of *nibbāna*.[8] In

1 Epictetus, *Dis.* II, 9:20–1. E. Schürer, *The History of the Jewish People in the Age of Jesus Christ (175 BC–AD 135)*, New English Version, III/1 (Edinburgh: Clark, 1986), 169, 173.

2 *Manu* 3:4. P.V. Kane, *History of Dharmasāstra* (Poona, Bhandarkar Institute, 1930–58), II/1 (1941), 408–9. One may be rejuvenated in water: W.D. O'Flaherty, *Asceticism and Eroticism in the Mythology of Siva* (London: Oxford University Press, 1973), 60–2.

3 Kane, *op.cit.*, II/2 (1941), 955, 958. Cf. *J* 5:7. For returning after penance: *Manu* 11:187, 190–1.

4 Josephus, *Antiquities* 18.116–19 at 118: baptism did *not* obtain pardon for sin. Cf. *Ac 22:16; 1Pe 3:21.*

5 Diogenes at Diogenes Laertius 6:42. *Anthol. Palat.* XIV,71cd (*Oxford Book of Greek Verse*, no.705). Philo, *Cherub.* 95–6; *Fug.*153 (cf. *Mt* 23:25); *Quod deus* 7–9. *Job* 9:30; *Jr* 2:22; *Ecclesiasticus* (Sirach) 31:30–1; Qumran scrolls, 1 QS III. 3–6; *H* 10:22; *P. Oxyr.* V.840.7–45; Ovid, *Fasti* 2.45–6; Seneca, *Hipp.* 715–18; *Her. Fur.* 918–19; Plato, *Sophist* 226D–228A; Justin, *Dial.* 13, 14, 44; Julian, *Against the Galileans* 245D Spanheim; Maimonides, *Guide of the Perplexed* III, 33 (trans. S. Pines, 1963/ 1974, 533–4); *Manu* 5:106; Tachibana, 164–5; Buddhaghosa, *Visuddhimagga* I.24. A. Oepke at *Theologisches Wörterbuch zum Neuen Testament* IV (1942), 303.13–17. R. Brown, *Body and Society* (Boston & London, 1988), 197–8, 333. M. Lambert, *Medieval Heresy* (London, 1977), 26.

6 *Manu* 11:124, 133, 150, 158, 175, 203, 215, 217, 224. Cf. *Miln* 2:212.

7 *Manu* 6:22, etc. Kane, *History* II/1, 658; II/2, 920. Cf. *Manu* 5:137. *D* 1:232–3; *A* 1:274, 2:219; *M* 1:335. 'Diving': Jātaka 6:377. Haripada Chakravarti, *Asceticism in Ancient India* (Calcutta: Punthi Pustak, 1973), 66. A. Wezler, 'A note on the class of ascetics called *unmajjaka*,' *Bulletin d'études indiennes* 9 (1991), 217–34. Cf. Juvenal, *Sat.* 6.522–4.

8 *A* 5:178, 180; *Ud* 1:9; *Therīgāthā* 236–51, trans. K.R. Norman, *Elders' Verses* II (London: Luzac, 1971), 26–7, 105–6. Jains had similar views. Schumann, 75–7.

his view the Eightfold Path is a 'lake' in which 'masters of lore' bathe and cross over to the shore of *nibbāna*.[1] Rivers cannot purify a man intent on evil deeds (*M 1:49–50*); but a defiled mind is rid of defilement when the subject *knows* it is defiled (*M1:46*), and one may cleanse oneself by abandoning the actions in question (*A 5:178*) (*see* pp. 123, 128 below).

Sprinkling or flicking with water is open to the same objections as immersion; and *abstaining* from washing, an ascetic practice, is just as much an observance (*Sn 249*) as immersing. There are washings which are pathological ruminations: the subject is deranged and what he/she does is of no significance.

---

1 *S* 1:232–3.

APPENDIX II

FORGIVENESS

IT cannot be claimed that the psychological processes whereby *X* believes himself to be forgiven by (a) God, or (b) a person whom he has wronged, are definitively worked out and described. It can be argued that preaching which concentrates on God's willingness to forgive offenders is unintentionally unhelpful, except to the guilt-ridden. To be persuaded that a former fault has been 'wiped out' (the metaphor of cleansing) can be a case of self-deception.

The ethical teachings of the Buddha and of Jesus had much in common, especially the great clue, viz. to renounce doing that which one hates to suffer from others. But the question of forgiveness can detain us. That we should forgive others as we wish to be forgiven ourselves makes sense and is in keeping with that 'clue'. But the teachers' positions on forgiveness are not identical. The Buddha did not forgive anyone. Buddhists do not ask for forgiveness, but something else having a similar effect. Jesus, on the other hand, following John the Baptist, asked sinners to repent, in the expectation of God's forgiveness.

Two questions are still unsettled:

1. Did Jesus himself forgive anyone? The Woman Taken in Adultery (*see* above p. 74) is not forgiven, only rescued. He speaks about forgiveness of certain of his patients who have suffered, and that may throw light on his personal power in relation to forgiveness. He announced that in certain cases forgiveness of sin had taken place, the passive voice being used to indicate that God had done it.[1] The implication is that Jesus knew whether God had forgiven a sinner who had suffered, and if his/her symptoms testified to God's wrath and these later abated there would be ground for such a conclusion. At *Mt 2:10* (cf. *9:8*) we are told Jesus had a delegated power to release sins on earth. The term 'release' arises from the Hebraic idea of binding and loosing as acts constituting or terminating the liability arising from a sin.[2] It is possible, furthermore, that Jesus, as a prophet, knew the sinner's standing otherwise than from the abatement of his/her malady. One can assert nothing about this, save that Jesus purported to know which single sin God would not forgive (*Mt 12:31–2*).

---

1 *Mk* 2:5–7; *L* 5:20–1, 7:47–8 (misunderstood at 49?). According to *Ps* 103:3 God heals all diseases and (therefore) forgives all sins.

2 Derrett, *SNT* 4: 190–5, also Neofiti Targum on *Lv* 4:20, 31; *Num* 14:19–21, 26–8, 30:6.

2. Was Jesus' method to require repentance before making any such pronouncement? A complicating factor is that he advised others to forgive without repentance (*Mt 18:22*), though Luke demurred here (*L 17:3*). It has been argued that Jesus' association with tax-gatherers and harlots, assumed to continue with their lucrative businesses, proved he did not require a prior repentance.[1] Alas, his 'treatment' of those 'sick' people would prove pointless if they did *not* repent! Jesus can have perceived that repentance is one thing, and social reinstatement another. He did not believe, any more than did the harlots, that to join the company of self-righteous people would be advantageous. However, the former lacked the respectability which their wealth had somehow failed to buy for them. Jesus offered them a new society. His version of the ancestral religion was concerned with the spiritual condition, and neither with membership of an existing social group, nor with the receipt of their money by synagogues (*Dt 23:18*) or by the Temple. Jesus would not take long to think of a charitable cause to which their donations *would* be acceptable (cf. *Mt 26:7; L 16:9*). Here are two aspects likely to annoy the Pharisees, who would recognize Jesus' want of enthusiasm for their own criteria.

Repentance would be met by forgiveness by God (*L 15:20*), since that was the position taken by the religion. Forgiveness was visualized as the remission of a debt, the debt was 'released'. In an a-theistical system such forgiveness was out of the question; and if belief in a 'self' was abandoned, that raised an additional difficulty. The Buddha's outlook is shown by an intriguing instance. The Hindu position, from which, no doubt, he had started out, was that a wrongdoer announced his fault as part of, or preparatory to, a penance or punishment.[2] The Buddha was not interested in punishment, though penance does figure by way of monastic discipline. Naturally this did not affect non-members of the *sangha*, though householder-believers would be aware of the principles. The leading case is that of Ajātasattu. He confessed to being a parricide. The Buddha replied:

> Truly, king, a fault has overcome you [the idiom for 'you have sinned'] according to your weakness, folly, and demerit, so that you put to death your father, a righteous man, a righteous ruler. And since you, king, confess [*disvā*, 'set out', 'proclaim'] you have committed a fault and make amends [*patikarosi*] according to *dhamma*, we accept [*patiganhāma*, not 'pardon'] it. For that, king, is propitious in the law of the 'noble ones', that whoever perceives he has committed a fault and makes amends [*patikaroti*] according to *dhamma*, achieves 'restraint' [*samvara*] for the future.[3]

The king was not subject to criminal jurisdiction, and the Buddha's (the *sangha's*)

---

1 E.P. Sanders, *Historical Figure* (1993), 230, 233. Derrett, *New Resolutions of Old Conundrums* (Shipston-on-Stour: Drinkwater, 1986), 142–8.

2 *Manu* 11:17, 83, 100, 104, 197.

3 *D* I: 94–5 (text *D* I: 85).

formula had no relevance to criminal liability. *Samvara* implies self-control, and propitious self-command. 'For restraint for the future' is part of the Buddhist confessional formula. When the ascetic Nigrodha was sarcastic at the Buddha's expense, and later showed contrition, the Buddha addressed him with the same formula as he used with Ajātasattu.[1]

This 'making amends' (*patikamma*) implies a (non-financial) compensation, a disclosure of remorse in order to re-establish fellowship. Some offences permit this procedure and some do not (*A 1:14*). An offence admits of *patikamma* where the monks hearing confession can restore the offending monk to his previous condition. Not 'pardon' but 'condonation' would be the better rendering. The hearers' *acceptance* (*patiggahana*) of the *patikamma* ('amends') is of the essence. Interestingly Luke (*23:42–3*) shows Jesus enthusiastically accepting the prayer of the converted thief at the point of death. He invites the former thief into his company in paradise.

The favourite disciple, Ananda's humility is reported at *Cl 379–80* (= *Cl XI.1, 10*, the Council at Rājagaha). Five times he was called upon by his seniors after the death of the Buddha to confess faults. In each case he gave an excuse, and that might well have been the end of the matter, but five disputes would have followed. He said he found no fault in his acts, but out of his faith [in his accusers] he 'made amends' *as if* they were faults. This was the Buddha's advice according to *Mv 2:209*. Whereas one should never accept as *dhamma* anything of which one does not personally approve, there may well be doubt how it is to be applied where an exact precedent of the Buddha's is not forthcoming. In such cases that which one's seniors define as a fault should be accepted as such (if with reservations) for the sake of comity. This position, typical of religious societies, could be extended only in the loosest sense to Ajātasattu, a lay, that is to say householder, supporter of the *sangha*, or to Nigrodha, who was not a supporter at all.

It is possible for a senior to 'forgive' a junior for his fault, and even to do so conditionally (*Miln 13–14*). But the word for 'forgive', *khamati*, basically means to be patient, or forbearing with someone or some thing. *Khanti* is 'forbearance' and, in that sense, forgiveness. To ask forgiveness of someone is *khamāpeti*, literally pacifying him or appeasing him, asking him to show *khanti*.

It seems as if Christian and Buddhist positions are irreconcilable; yet the differences are superficial. The two systems agree that disburdenment by the wrongdoer, as evidence of his/her contrition, affects in unseen ways his/her status as wrongdoer: so supersensory ills, in this life or another, are counteracted. This is a religious position, but none the less the fruit of observation of people's sensations and behaviour. The objection to confession and absolution, that these do not necessarily reform behaviour, is met by the comment that unreflecting or insincere confession is no disburdenment.

---

1 *D 3:50*. Cf. *BD 2:199–200*.

The position adopted in the Mahāyāna, that the Buddhist confesses before all Buddhas and compassionate Bodhisattvas, expressing remorse and undertaking never more to do 'unholy work', the Masters taking the transgression as it is,[1] is not traceable to Christian influence. The Buddhas and Bodhisattvas, true to the Theravāda tradition, do not forgive anyone.

The medieval discovery that the Virgin Mother of Christ both could and would intercede with her Son on behalf of sinners was one of the great religious discoveries of all time. She no longer guaranteed, merely, the genuineness of her son's birth and Resurrection; she also provided solace for inadequate professors of the Christian religion: hence the immense flowering, due to clerical patronage, of the arts depicting the Madonna and Child.

---

1 Sāntideva, *Bodhicaryāvatāra*, ch. 2 (trans. L.D. Barnett, *The Path of Light* [London: Murray, 1909], 40–43).

APPENDIX III

THE SECRET

THE discovery made by Gotama the Buddha and by Jesus of Nazareth was one and the same, though 'cocooned' in different idioms and verbiage. The result can be stated as a 'rule', and two illustrations will serve.

1. From all that you hate withdraw.
   a. Withdraw negatively, by not resisting the thought/speech/action of the other party.
   b. Withdraw positively, (i) by not thinking/speaking/acting in that way against any other person (or group); (ii) by practising in thought (etc.) the reverse.
2. That done, you freely act as a moral person, free of blame, freely acquiring merit.
3. Illustration 1: arrogance.
   a. Do not respond negatively to the arrogance of X, decline to be a target for it.
   b. Do not think/speak/act arrogantly to any person; act humbly towards all.
4. Illustration 2: physical violence (which Gotama and Jesus chose as their paradigm).
   a. Do not resist the violence of X, decline to be its victim.
   b. Neither provoke violence, nor exert violence upon others.
5. This gives freedom to you, though not immediately to X; but the teaching is subjective: it aims at X's victim. One acquires merit by not evincing counter-arrogance or counter-violence.
6. The condition of X, which induces him to seek victims for arrogance, or violence, is not dealt with by the Masters. They do not speculate to explain, or mitigate, the behaviour of X, but we guess that the strategy will indirectly cure X.

The insight required for this discovery is supported by the Golden Rule, one of the oldest pieces of human wisdom.[1] To adopt it is to employ one's autonomy. It needs no religion to support it, nor is the arbitrament of the 'ideal observer' resorted to. *See* commentators on *Mt 7:12*.

To escape post-death pains or to gain post-death bliss, granted the possibility of reincarnation, was hoped for in the ancient world. But that a 'conversion', and

1 *See* p. 70 §8 above. Dihle (1962); A. Nissen, *Gott und Nächste* (1974), 390–9, 402; P. Ricoeur, 'The Golden Rule', *NTS* 36/3 (1990), 392–7.

not some mystical mumbo-jumbo, could cure all was new (cf. Plato, *Phaedo*, 69C–70D). Both primitive Buddhism and primitive Christianity assumed that the mental impressions of enlightenment would survive the death of the enlightened one, and would be effective to his advantage thereafter (*J 11:25–6*).

FURTHER READING

Indicates works which are relatively popular and accessible

BUDDHISM

The Buddha's Life and Background

T.W. Rhys Davids. *Buddhist India* (London, 1903; Calcutta, 1950/1959).

*E.J. Thomas. *The Life of Buddha as Legend and History* (London, 1927/1975).

N. Wagle. *Society at the Time of the Buddha* (Bombay, 1966).

J.M. Kitagawa and M.D. Cummings. *Buddhism and Asian History* (New York: Macmillan; London: Collins, 1989).

*M. Carrithers. *The Buddha* (Past Master Series; Oxford: University Press, 1983).

One may refer to:
*W. Doniger and Brian K. Smith. *The Laws of Manu* (London: Penguin, 1991).

*R.C. Zaehner, trans., *Hindu Scriptures* (London: Dent, 1966) (it includes the Bhagavadgītā).

I recommend:
*H.W. Schumann. *The Historical Buddha* (London: Arkana, 1989).

also:
*A.L. Basham. *The Wonder that was India* (London: Sidgwick & Jackson, 1954, and constantly reprinted).

Indian Buddhism

E. Frauwallner. *The Earliest Vinaya and the Beginnings of Buddhist Literature* (Ser. Or. Roma 8; Rome: IsMEO, 1956).

*N.A. Nigam and R. McKeon. *The Edicts of Asoka* (Chicago & London: University of Chicago Press, 1966).

Bhikshu Sangharakshita. *The Three Jewels. An Introduction to Buddhism* (London: Rider, 1967).

Bhikshu Sangharakshita. 'Buddhism', in A.L. Basham, ed., *A Cultural History of India* (Oxford: Clarendon Press, 1975), 83–99.

E Lamotte. *Histoire du Bouddhisme Indien* (Publ. Inst. Or. Louvain 14; Louvain-la-Neuve: Institut Orientaliste, 1976).

Hajime Nakamura. *Indian Buddhism. A Survey with Bibliographical Notes* (Delhi: Motilal Banarsidass, 1987/1989).

*Richard F. Gombrich. *Theravāda Buddhism. A Social History from Ancient Benares to Modern Colombo* (London, etc.: Routledge, 1988).

Ulrich Schneider. *Die Grossen Felsen-Edikte Asokas* (Wiesbaden: Harrassowitz, 1978).

Buddhism

S. Bernard-Thierry. 'Le bouddhisme d'après les textes pālis,' in R. de Berval, ed., *Présence de Bouddhisme* (*France-Asie*, 16, nos. 153–7 [1959], 571–632).

Richard A. Gard, ed. *Buddhism* (London: Prentice Hall; New York: Braziller, 1961).

*Richard H. Robinson. *The Buddhist Religion. A Historical Introduction* (Belmont,CA: Dickens, 1970 [bibliography]).

*T. Ling. *The Buddha. Buddhist Civilization in India and Ceylon* (Harmondsworth: Penguin, 1976).

*T. Ling. ed. *The Buddha's Philosophy of Man. Early Indian Buddhist Dialogues* (London: Dent, Everyman, 1981).

Peter Harvey. *An Introduction to Buddhism: Teachings, History and Practice* (Cambridge: University Press, 1990) (a comprehensive work).

also:

M.E. Spiro. *Buddhism and Society. A Great Tradition and its Burmese Vicissitudes* (Berkeley: University of California Press, 1971).

H. Bechert. *Buddhismus. Staat und Gesellschaft in den Ländern des Theravada Buddhismus*, vol. 1 (Frankfurt, 1966); vols. 2–3 (Wiesbaden, 1967, 1973).

P. Olivelle. *The Origin and Early Development of Buddhist Monachism* (Colombo, 1974).

René Gothóni. 'Caste and kinship within Sinhalese Buddhist monasticism,' in A. Parpola and B.S. Hansen, edd., *South Asian Religion and Society* (Scand. Inst. As. St., *Studies on Asian Topics* 11; London: Curzon; Riverdale, MD: Riverdale Co., 1986).

A magnificent survey of religion and art:
*H. Bechert and R. Gombrich, edd., *The World of Buddhism. Buddhist Monks and Nuns in Society and Culture* (London: Thames & Hudson, 1984).

R. de Berval. *Présence de Bouddhisme* (Paris: Gallimard, 1987).

R. Lingat. *Royautés bouddhiques* (Paris: École des Hautes Études en Sciences Sociales, 1989).

S.J. Tambiah. *Buddhism Betrayed? Religion, Politics and Violence in Sri Lanka* (Chicago & London: University of Chicago Press, 1992).

Buddhist Ethics

An excellent classical exposition:
Peter Gerlitz, 'Die Ethik des Buddha,' in C.H. Ratschow, ed., *Ethik der Religionen. Ein Handbuch* (Stuttgart: Kohlhammer, 1980), 227–348. The study by the same in A. Th. Khoury, ed., *Das Ethos der Weltreligionen* (Freiburg, etc.: Herder, 1993) has the advantage of appearing in association with a study of Christian ethics by F. Fulger.

*S. Tachibana. *The Ethics of Buddhism* [1926] (London, etc.: Curzon Press, 1981).

L. de La Vallée Poussin. *Le dogme et la philosophie du Bouddhisme* (Brussels, 1930).

C.A.F. Rhys Davids. *A Buddhist Manual of Psychological Ethics* [1900] (London, 3rd edn., 1974).

C.A.F. Rhys Davids. *Buddhism. A Study of the Buddhist Norm* (London: Williams & Norgate, 1912).

F. E. Reynolds. 'Buddhist ethics,' *Religious Studies Review* 5/1 (1979), 47ff.

I recommend:

*H. Saddhatissa. *Buddhist Ethics. Essence of Buddhism* (London: George Allen, 1970).

*Walpola Rahula. *What the Buddha Taught*, revised edn. (London, etc.: Gordon Fraser, 1967/1978).

I.B. Horner. *The Early Buddhist Theory of Man Perfected* [1936] (Amsterdam: Philo, 1975).

J.T. Ergardt. *Faith and Knowledge in Early Buddhism* (Leiden: Brill, 1977).

Harvey B. Aronson. *Love and Sympathy in Theravāda Buddhism* (Delhi: M. Banarsidass, 1980).

S. Collins. *Selfless Persons. Imagery and Thought in Theravāda Buddhism* (Cambridge: University Press, 1982).

Y. Hoffmann. *The Idea of Self – East and West. A Comparison between Buddhist Philosophy and the Philosophy of David Hume* (Calcutta: Firma KLM, 1980).

C. Oetke. *'Ich' und das Ich. Analytische Untersuchungen zur buddhistisch-brahmanische Atmankontroverse* (Wiesbaden: Steiner, 1988).

Bodhisattvas

Har Dayal. *The Bodhisattva Doctrine in Buddhist Sanskrit Literature* (London: Kegan Paul, 1932).

Akira Hirakawa. 'The Rise of Mahāyān Buddhism...stūpas', *Mem. Res. Dep. Tokyo Bunko* 22 (1963), 57–106.

Leslie S. Kawamura. *The Bodhisattva Doctrine in Buddhism* (SR Suppl. 10; Waterloo, Ont.: Laurier University, 1981).

*Paul Williams, *Mahāyāna Buddhism. The Doctrinal Foundations* (London, etc.: Routledge, 1989).

David S. Ruegg. *Buddha-nature, Mind, and the Problem of Gradualism in a Comparative Perspective* (London: School of Oriental & African Studies, 1989).

*Beatrice L. Suzuki. *Mahayana Buddhism* [1938], 4th edn. (London: Unwin Paperbacks, 1990).

Special Topics

B. Gokhale. 'The early Buddhist view of the state,' *J. Am. Oriental Society* 89 (1969), 731ff.

T. Ling. *Buddhism, Imperialism and War* (London: Allen & Unwin, 1979).

Lambert Schmithausen. *The Problem of Sentience of Plants in Earliest Buddhism* (Studia Philologica Buddhica, Mono. 6; Tokyo: International Institute for Buddhist Studies, 1991).

Lambert Schmithausen. *Buddhism and Nature* (St. Phil. Budd., Mono.7; Tokyo: Int. Inst. Buddh. St., 1991).

Christopher K. Chapple. *Nonviolence to Animals, Earth and Self in Asian Traditions* (Albany, NY: State University of New York Press, 1993).

Comparative

R.C.F. Aiken. *The Dhamma of Gotama the Buddha and the Gospel of Jesus the Christ* (Boston: Marlier, 1900).

J. Boyd. *Satan and Māra. Christian and Buddhist Symbols of Evil* (SHR 27; Leiden: Brill, 1975).

Gustav Mensching. *Buddha und Christus – ein Vergleich* (Stuttgart: Deutsche Verlags-Anstalt, 1978).

*Daisetsu T. Suzuki. *Mysticism Christian and Buddhist* (London: Unwin Paperbacks, 1979).

F. Buri. *Der Buddha-Christus als der Herr des wahren Selbst* (Bern, etc.: Paul Haupt, 1982).

Vincent L. Wimbush and R. Valantasis, edd. *Asceticism* (New York: Oxford University Press, 1995).

CHRISTIANITY

Judaism

H. Danby. *The Mishnah* (London: Oxford University Press, 1933).

G.F. Moore. *Judaism*, 3 vols. (Cambridge, MA: Harvard University Press, 1958).

W.D. Davies. *The Setting of the Sermon on the Mount* (Cambridge: University Press, 1964).

*J.D.M. Derrett. *Jesus's Audience* (London: Darton, Longman & Todd, 1973).

A. Nissen. *Gott und der Nächste im antiken Judentum* (Tübingen: Mohr, 1974).

J. Neusner and others, edd. *Judaisms and Their Messiahs at the Turn of the Christian Era* (Cambridge: University Press, 1987).

A. Büchler. *Types of Jewish-Palestinian Piety from 70 BCE to 70 CE. The Ancient Pious Men* (London: Jews' College, 1922).

*M.A. Knibb. *The Qumran Community* (Cambridge: University Press, 1987).

G. Vermes and M.G. Goodman. *The Essenes According to the Classical Sources* (Sheffield: Academic Press, 1989).

J. Hastings. 'Therapeutae', in J. Hastings, ed., *Encyclopaedia of Religion and Ethics* (Edinburgh: T.& T. Clark, 1908–26), XII, 315–19.

C. Milikowsky. 'Which Gehenna…?', *NTS* 34 (1988), 238–49 (resurrection for the *just*).

Jesus

D. Flusser. *Jesus* (Reinbek: Rowohlt, 1968).

J. Dupont. *Les tentations de Jésus au désert* (SN 4; Bruges: Desclée de Brouwer, 1968).

G. Vermes. *Jesus the Jew. A Historical Reading of the Gospels* (London: Collins, 1973).

S. Westerholm. *Jesus and Scribal Authority* (Lund: Gleerup, 1978).

P. Lapide and U. Luz. *Der Jude Jesus. Thesen eines Juden. Antworten eines Christen* (Zürich: Benziger, 1987).

E. Bammel and C.F.D. Moule, edd. *Jesus and the Politics of his Day* (Cambridge: University Press, 1984).

Rainer Riesner. *Jesus als Lehrer* (*WUNT* 2/7; Tübingen: Mohr, 1st edn. 1981, 2nd edn. 1984).

*Ian Wilson. *Jesus. The Evidence* (London: Book Club, 1984).

*J. Alison. *Knowing Jesus* (London: SPCK, 1993).

*G. Vermes. *The Religion of Jesus the Jew* (London, SCM Press, 1993).

*E.P. Sanders. *The Historical Figure of Jesus* (London: Allen Lane, 1993).

*N.T. Wright. *Who Was Jesus?* (Grand Rapids, MI: Eerdmans, 1993) (demolishes several fanciful biographies of Jesus).

The New Testament

C.F.D. Moule. *Man and Nature in the New Testament* (London: Athlone Press, 1964), reprinted in Facet Books, Biblical Series 17 (Philadelphia: Fortress Press, 1967).

W.D. Davies. *Invitation to the New Testament. A Guide to Its Main Witnesses* (London: Darton, Longman & Todd, 1967).

*A.E. Harvey. *Companion to the New Testament* (Oxford & Cambridge: University Presses, 1970).

W. Horbury and B. McNeil. edd. *Suffering and Martyrdom in the New Testament* (Cambridge: University Press, 1981).

*E. Charpentier. *How to Read the New Testament* (London: SCM Press, 1981).

*John E. Stambaugh and D.L. Balch. *The New Testament in its Social Environment* (Philadelphia: Westminster, 1986).

B.M. Metzger and M.D.Coogan, edd. *Oxford Companion to the Bible* (New York & Oxford: Oxford University Press, 1993).

Christian Ethics

A. Dihle. *Die goldene Regel. Eine Einführung in die Geschichte der antiken und frühchristlichen Vulgärethik* (Göttingen: Vendenhoeck & Ruprecht, 1962) .

J. Ferguson. *Moral Values in the Ancient World* (London: Methuen, 1958).

P. Pokorny. *Der Kern der Bergpredigt. Eine Auslegung* (Hamburg, 1969).

W.S. Kissinger. *The Sermon on the Mount. A History of Interpretation and Bibliography* (Metuchen, NJ, 1975) .

R.J. Cassidy. *Jesus, Politics, and Society* (Maryknoll, NY: Orbis, 1978).

J. Piper. *'Love Your Enemies'* (Cambridge: University Press, 1979).

(Sir) Norman Anderson. *The Teaching of Jesus* (London: Hodder & Stoughton, 1983) .

*H. Hendrickx. *The Sermon on the Mount* (Waco, TX, 1984).

A. Verhey. *The Great Reversal. Ethics of the New Testament* (Grand Rapids, MI: Eerdmans, 1984).

Thomas W. Ogletree. *The Use of the Bible in Christian Ethics* (Oxford: Blackwell, 1984).

U. Berner. *Die Bergpredigt. Rezeption und Auslegungen im 20. Jahrhundert* (Göttingen: Vandenhoeck & Ruprecht, 3rd edn. 1985).

Charles L. Cohen. *God's Caress: the Psychology of Puritan Religious Experience* (New York: Oxford University Press, 1986).

Celia Deutsch. *Hidden Wisdom and the Easy Yoke* (JSNTS 18; Sheffield: Academic Press, 1987).

T.E. Schmidt. *Hostility to Wealth in the Synoptic Gospels* (JSNTS 15; Sheffield: Academic Press, 1987).

M.J. Borg. *Conflict, Holiness and Politics in the Teaching of Jesus* (Toronto: Mellen, 1984).

G. Strecker. *The Sermon on the Mount. An Exegetical Commentary* (EV; Edinburgh: T. & T. Clark, 1988).

W. Schrage. *Ethics of the New Testament* (EV; Edinburgh: T & T Clark, 1988).

*A.E. Harvey. *Strenuous Commands. The Ethic of Jesus* (London: SCM Press, 1990).

W. Crockett, ed. *Four Views on Hell* (Grand Rapids, MI: Zondervan, 1992).

*J.D.M. Derrett. *The Sermon on the Mount. A Manual for Living* (Northampton: Pilkington, 1994).

J.H. Yoder. *The Politics of Jesus*, 2nd edn. (Carlisle: Paternoster Press, 1994).

Also:

H.H. Henson. *Christian Morality. Natural, Developing, Final* (Oxford: Clarendon Press, 1936).

A.R. Osborn. *Christian Ethics* (London, etc.: Oxford University Press, 1940).

Arthur W.H. Adkins. *Merit and Responsibility* (Oxford: University Press, 1960).

J.B. Russell. *The Devil: Perceptions of Evil from Antiquity to Primitive Christianity* (Ithaca, NY: Cornell University Press, 1977).

Alan Gewirth. *Reason and Morality* (Chicago: University of Chicago Press, 1978).

James M. Gustafson. *Theology and Ethics* (Oxford: Blackwell, 1981), esp. ch. 1–2.

L.C.M. Fairweather and J.I.H. McDonald. *The Quest for Christian Ethics* (Edinburgh: Handsel, 1984).

*R.G. Jones. *Groundwork of Christian Ethics* (London: Epworth, 1984).

Robin Gill. *A Textbook of Christian Ethics* (Edinburgh: T.& T. Clark, 1985).

D.O. Via. *The Ethics of Mark's Gospel* (Philadelphia: Fortress Press, 1985).

*Charles L. Kammer. *Ethics and Literature: an Introduction* (London: SCM Press. 1988).

O. Cullmann. *Baptism in the New Testament* (SBT 1; London: SCM Press, 1950/1956).

Allen D. Verhey. 'Ethical lists', 'Ethics', in: B.M. Metzger and M.D. Coogan, edd., *Oxford Companion to the Bible* (New York & Oxford: Oxford University Press, 1993), 201–5.

*F.R.J. Williams. *Science and a Global Ethic* (Northampton: Pilkington, 1994).

*A.E. Harvey. *Promise or Pretence?* (London: SCM Press, 1994).

On the question whether religion is indispensable for morality, see (for a negative response) essays in:

Bert Musschenga, ed. *Does Religion Matter Morally? A Critical Reappraisal of the Thesis of Morality's Independence from Religion* (Morality and the Meaning of Life 3; Kampen: Pharos, 1994).

INDEX